Published 2020

Printed in the United States of America
Print ISBN: 978-1-951490-38-6

Canoe Tree Press
4697 Main Street
Manchester Center, VT 05255

Canoe Tree Press is the self-publishing imprint of DartFrog Books

www.CanoeTreePress.com

YOU JUST CAN'T MAKE THIS STUFF UP...

THE TRIALS AND TRIUMPHS OF NEGOTIATING MERGERS AND ACQUISITIONS

Jay M. Bylsma and Randy Rua

ALSO BY JAY M. BYLSMA

FICTION

"Pitcher's Hands is Out" with Dan Bylsma
"Slam Dunks Are Not Allowed" with Dan Bylsma
"The Reprobate"

NON-FICTION

"So Your Son Wants to Play in the NHL" with Dan Bylsma
"So You Want to Play in the NHL" with Dan Bylsma

FOREWORD

To paraphrase the announcer on the radio and television show *Dragnet*, the stories you are about to read are true; the names have been changed to protect the guilty. We have been intermediaries or business brokers collectively for over 80 years and have been involved with literally hundreds of deals. Some were successful, others less so. Some were long, drawn-out affairs with every figure and word scrutinized endlessly by one lawyer or accountant after another. Others seemed to happen overnight. But all were interesting, and some were memorable.

The ones we have included in this book are the memorable ones. They are the ones that prompted us to say about the deal, or what transpired to make it come off successfully or go down in flames, "You just can't make this stuff up."

So, it follows that none of the stories in this work are made up. There is an actual deal or experience behind all this fiction. The names, companies, product lines, and dates have been changed to protect the confidentiality to which we are committed and also to protect the innocent and to excoriate the guilty, albeit anonymously.

Being an intermediary is a fun ride and highly satisfying. To be entrusted with the sale of one's life work or the purchase of a new life endeavor is a high honor and a trust we take very seriously.

We undertook to write a primer in how to buy or sell a business and to show its potential pitfalls as a work of fiction because we both believe truth is sometimes best told in fiction. Besides, fiction can be made far more interesting than a "How-To" treatise. Believe us, we tried the treatise route, and reading it cured one of us of our insomnia.

There is a popular book in the bookstores, *The Art of the Deal*, recently made more popular by national election events. Neither of us ever met Art, and he never showed up to make our deals easier to put together. In fact, there has never been an easy one, and we sell part of our central nervous system with each one. This is largely not because of some creative deal-making process of which we are unaware but because of the human condition, which includes such characteristics as belligerence, death, distrust, divorce, gamesmanship, greed . . . and we're only in the 'G's alphabetically. Someone once asked if a degree in corporate finance was a pre-requisite to becoming an intermediary, to which our response is always is, "No, get a PhD in Psychology."

The stories are divided into two sections. We call the first section "The Twenty Percent" for reasons that will be explained when you get to the section called "The Eighty Percent."

So, enjoy. If you find a story that parallels your experience with either of us, know that you are probably wrong, but if not, we won't tell if you won't.

     Jay M. Bylsma   *Randy Rua*

SECTION ONE

THE TWENTY PERCENT

CHAPTER ONE

SOMETIME IN 1980

*"Working hard for someone with the expectation
you can take over the business when he retires
almost always hardly ever works."* **–Randy Rua**

It was his path to success and perhaps even wealth. James Harrington ("Harry" to his friends and fellow employees) had worked at Dyno Machine, Inc. for 15 years, beginning as a machine operator. Being able to think and act on his feet caused him to be promoted to Inside Sales and Engineering. Completing his B.S. degree in Mechanical Engineering going to night school had propelled him to VP of Engineering and as Jim Bateman, the owner, approached retirement, Harry had assumed the duties of General Manager.

He was clearly being groomed to take over the company. He and his wife of 12 years had lived frugally, (more frugally than Lisa wanted to live) so Harry could save enough money for at least a down payment when the time came and the company could be his.

So, one can only imagine how high Harry's hopes soared when Mr. Bateman took him aside and announced he was ready to retire and, with a twinkle in his eye, indicated his plans for succession included Harry in a very special place, a place Bateman had been mentoring him for several years now. "You have exceeded all the expectations I've ever had for you, Harry, and I'm very proud of how far you've come. With you here, I can sail into the sunset of retirement with every confidence," were his parting words as the meeting concluded.

So, tonight was going to be his night. A Jerry Garcia tie over a blue shirt was worn with a freshly dry-cleaned and pressed suit. "You look terrific," Lisa said as she straightened the tie. "And I'm so proud of you." The dress she wore was a bit too sexy, but she was an attractive woman—why not show off a little of what she had? And with some final words for the babysitter, they were off to the Bateman retirement party.

The country club ballroom was elegant enough, so no decorations were needed. For most of the thirty-five employees this would be the first and only time they would experience how the "other half" enjoyed their free time. The invitation's instructions of "tie and jacket required" was misinterpreted by some who wondered why a jacket was required on a warm summer evening and there was but a handful of Windsor knots to be seen.

Many of the hourly workers drifted toward Harry. He was seen as one of theirs who had beaten the odds and "made it." They were as pleased as Harry that he would be their new leader. He was someone who had been one of them, who would and could understand them and their interests and needs. When dinner was served, there had been enough adult beverages consumed to put everyone at ease with their surroundings, and the expectations for the future were high.

The fact that Mr. Bateman had invited his only son and daughter-in-law to share in his retirement party seemed entirely appropriate.

***

As ebullient as they were on the way to the party, they were equally disheartened on the ride home. He wondered how many people noticed his look of shock (or was it disgust?) when Bateman announced he would be turning the presidency over to his son, a recent Harvard Business School grad, under the capable mentoring of the ever-faithful James Harrington.

She wondered if and when he could recover from the shock.

They rode in silence. He was afraid to talk lest he break into tears or a rage.

She was afraid to talk because she knew nothing she could say would mollify his disappointment and grief.

CHAPTER TWO

SOMETIME IN 1982

"Working for someone else is one of the best ways to prepare yourself for starting your own business." –Jay M. Bylsma

H arry took a new interest in the trade journals that came to Dyno Machine. These magazines carried stories of new technology coming into the industry, success stories about machine shops that had risen to new heights of sales or competence, stories about giants in the industry who were retiring, and ads for equipment for sale. It was the ads for equipment for sale that captured his attention.

There were two things that kept him from resigning from Dyno: his need for a regular paycheck and the cost of the good equipment he would need to start his own business. A small 3-axis CNC vertical machining center was over $50,000 new and $35,000 used—if you could find something that was low mileage. That would give you a start. All told, it would take an excess of $500,000 to equip a shop properly with the necessary machines and ancillary equipment. And then there was the office equipment. While he had some of that saved up, he would have to borrow heavily, and if he were candid, both he and Lisa were debt adverse.

But "babysitting," as Harry thought of tending to his new boss, was becoming ever more intolerable. The young college graduate saw every issue as a Harvard Business School case study to be endlessly discussed. Did there really need to be a committee meeting to decide whether it would be appropriate to include organic food in the vending machines? There was no doubt the kid would become a good businessman over time, but in the meantime, there was a lot of Harry's time being wasted while more pressing matters were being unnecessarily postponed. To be sure, the new president did implement some changes that were needed. He authored an employee manual outlining benefits, tardiness, and absentee policies, and a Confidentiality Agreement and Covenant Not to Compete. He also started a monthly newsletter introducing new employees, highlighting birthdays and anniversaries, and announcing policy changes and new customers.

Conversely, some of the customer service policies, like providing free drawings and first part pre-shipment approvals had been thought of by the president as unnecessary and were eliminated. Everything was about leading by control and management by exception—and while it had not cost the company any customers, and the company's margins had improved somewhat, the company's previous relationships, which could have been described as "cozy," were becoming a bit more formal, sometimes strained. The kid was not the old man yet. And Harry didn't feel like he could stay around until the kid's "yet" happened.

So, he took the trade journals home and pored over the used machinery sales pages and scoured the Internet for bargains. Over the next six months, he bought a piece here and a piece there, and his two-car garage began to fill up while his savings filled down.

It was a phone call from an old standby customer that tipped the scales in favor of his leaving Dyno. The bid for machining a rather complicated aluminum die cast part had not been responded to for too long, so Harry called the customer.

"Ben! Harry at Dyno calling. How've you been? Good, thanks. I saw your youngest at a soccer game last Saturday, and he's good. Congratulations! Listen I'm calling about our bid on that aluminum die cast part. We're able to start on it right away. Have you made a decision to go ahead with it?"

The excuses were those Harry had begun to hear from other customers who had taken their business elsewhere: the need for a second source of supply, the price was not competitive, the delivery was not what they could have expected in the past, and the service is not the same since Junior took over.

"The company's not the same under the new ownership" was something about which Harry could do nothing.

And so he handed in his resignation, and CORE Machining, Inc. was born. Harry would be quick to answer anyone's question as to what the CORE stood for: "Customer Oriented Relationships Exemplified."

One mistake the previous owner of Dyno Machine made was not buying Harry a cell phone, but in a thoughtless cost-saving measure, he reimbursed Harry $30.00 a month to use his personal phone. This meant that all of Harry's business contacts contacted him on his personal cell phone, and his business card carried his personal cell phone number.

On advice of his attorney, Harry could answer the phone with "CORE Machining"; however, to be extra cautious, he could choose to answer the phone with his given name. And when the call concerned old, current, or new business with Dyno, Harry was instructed to say, "I'm sorry, I'm not employed at Dyno Machine any longer. You will have to call them about your business." Because most of Dyno Machining customers were on a first name basis with Harry, they almost always asked what he was doing. Only if specifically asked as to what he was doing now should he say that he had started his own business. Then, only if specifically asked as to what the new business did should he say, "I've opened my own machine shop. I appreciate your interest, call me back sometime and we'll see if there is any way I could help you."

And call back they usually did. And so did Dyno Machine, Inc's lawyers.

CHAPTER THREE

LATER IN 1982

"Having a good lawyer is the most expensive and best thing that can happen to you." **–Randy Rua**

Harry had never been asked by Dyno Machine to sign the Confidentiality Agreement, and he had been careful never to call a customer of Dyno. But the loss of business to Dyno because of the relationships Harry had established over several years and his position as the face of Dyno to their customers was beginning to make an adverse difference to Dyno's sales and bottom line and a positive impact on CORE. The Harvard Business School grad would have none of it, and so the letter from Dyno's attorneys. It contained a laundry list of alleged infractions including theft of company secrets, being in violation of the Covenant Not To Compete, violation of the Confidentiality Agreement, theft of company property, improper interference with customer relationships, and others.

The queasy feeling you get in the pit of your stomach when

there are the flashing red lights of a police car intending to pull you over, or you get a letter from opposing counsel, came to Harry's. Lisa's reaction was borderline panic. They both went to see their lawyer the next day.

After settling in at the lawyer's office, he said, "Let's take their allegations one by one. What secrets are there in a machine shop? That is, does Dyno have any proprietary knowledge or secrets, that is knowledge that is not common to any other machine shop?"

"None that I know of, except perhaps their customer list."

"Do their customers know they're on that list?"

"I suppose so."

"Then that's not a secret that could have been stolen."

"Did you sign either a Covenant Not to Compete or a Confidentiality Agreement?"

"No, there are these documents in the Employee Manual, but I was never asked to sign them."

"Their contention is going to be that, it being in the Employee Manual, there is an implied contract between Dyno and the employee. However, in law, a contract that can be changed by one party, in this case the employer, without the consent of the other party is not an enforceable contract. So, their claim of violation of the Covenant Not to Compete and the Confidentiality Agreement is baseless and nothing more than a scare tactic. Do you have any idea what company property they could claim you have stolen?"

"They paid for part of my cell phone bill because I used it for company business."

"In whose name was the phone registered and to what address was the phone bill sent?"

"It is my phone, it's registered to me, the bill comes to my home, and I pay the bill. Dyno reimbursed me $30.00 a month.

"If that's what they're talking about, it is not theft to have possession of something that is registered to you and for what you pay for. As regards 'improper interference with customer relationships,' you could have answered your phone as "CORE Machining," but you were more conservative. You also didn't need to instruct your callers to call Dyno after you said you didn't work for them anymore, and you did. It goes without saying that you were more circumspect than the law allows. They have no basis for a claim against you."

"So how should we respond to their letter?"

"I suggest I write them back indicating I've reviewed your actions as it relates to the law, that their claims are baseless and amount to nothing more than scare tactics and intimidation, and that any further action they take to interfere with the lawful operation of your business will be responded to in the strongest possible terms. And they will leave you alone. I know their attorneys, and they're good lawyers. They're being advocates for Dyno's new president, but they also know this a fight they can't win. If they were to sue you on these charges, we'd win in Summary Judgment and they know it."

It was Lisa's turn to ask a question, "What is Summary Judgment?"

"It means we would petition the trial judge to dismiss their case before it ever came to trial."

Harry returned to the loft where his three employees were machining parts and never looked back. Lisa went home relieved and looked forward to Harry's continued success.

CHAPTER FOUR

"A star is born . . ." –Jay M. Bylsma

D avid McTavish was a junior accountant in a local CPA firm when he had his first chance to shine. He had an MBA from the University of Michigan in accounting and finance but was in the "bull pen"—a large room of desks where six other recent accounting graduates did personal tax returns and the grunt work of audit procedures. He happened to overhear a partner of the firm bemoan that one of his clients had been approached to sell his business and needed an opinion of the value. But no one in the firm had any expertise in valuing closely held companies. It would have to be hired out to a competing firm, which the partner was loath to do.

After less than ten seconds of serious consideration, McTavish left his desk, approached the partner, and told him of his experience in such valuations. He explained to the skeptical partner that Morgan Collins, former Asst. Treasurer of Ford Motor Company, was his Advance Corporate Finance professor and had spent considerable time with valuation methods for closely held companies.

McTavish would like the opportunity to help the firm and have a chance to do the valuation.

It was decided to farm the valuation out but also give McTavish a chance to "see how close he could come" to a professional valuation. And shine he did by coming within 5% of the outside firm's opinion of value and 2% of what the business actually sold for.

McTavish shone in other ways and rose through the ranks of the firm until one of his clients lured him away to become a part owner, treasurer, and member of the board of directors in a rapidly growing industrial equipment firm—Construct, Inc.

Within a year of his arrival at the new job, the firm was approached by a NYSE firm looking to solidify their base in Michigan. Valuation was a problem in the negotiations, but McTavish was able to convince the buyer that the price for growth required a premium multiplier. The purchase of the new subsidiary was soon justified by Construct, Inc. providing only 3% of the parent's sales but 10% of its net income.

With the subsidiary's continued success, McTavish's star continued to shine, and he was called in to assist the parent in negotiating another acquisition. And another—this one in Italy.

Then lightning struck. The parent company was purchased by a German conglomerate who decided his subsidiary was in competition with one of their sales outlets, and Construct, Inc. was selected to be closed. Fortunately, McTavish had a golden parachute in his employment contract, and he walked out the door with a one-year severance package at full salary and benefits.

A month later, at the weekly Rotary Club meeting, he chanced to sit next to an attorney acquaintance who was having a bad day. The attorney indicated he represented the seller in a business transaction that should go together but wouldn't. Over the rubber chicken entrée, the French-dressing salad, and a very hard roll, he complained he had been working on the deal for two months and the acquisition had a potential of being good for both sides, but that morning it was like trying to keep magnets with opposite poles to connected.

McTavish only said, "I can relate."

The attorney slowly turned to him. "McTavish? MacTavish. You did the Construct merger, didn't you?"

"Yes, and several others."

"Are you still with Construct?"

"No. I'm taking a year off. Construct was closed due to my being successful in another acquisition, and my unexpected departure was 'golden,' you might say."

The attorney thought a moment and then said, "I'd like to call you when I get back to the office."

"Please do. I'd be happy to help if I can."

***

The attorney did call, and McTavish went to see if he could help. McTavish had long learned a merger or acquisition is like a puzzle. Only when all the pieces fit does the complete picture emerge. With fresh eyes, McTavish saw an extended warranty was needed here, a premium for this or that was needed there, this needed to be expanded and that contracted or removed, and a life insurance policy on one of the principals was needed to make the pieces fit. In three weeks, the deal was closed.

"This area could use someone with your background and experience." It was the attorney addressing McTavish. "As attorneys, too often we are either too close to the situation or too protective of our client to see what needs to happen to make the deal close. I could have used you several times in the past few years. You should think about setting out a shingle."

McTavish did think about it. But a few weeks later, a letter came in his mailbox from the State Department of Licensing. There had been a complaint filed by a local real estate agent that McTavish was unlicensed and had taken a fee for the sale of real estate or goodwill for which a real estate license was required. He had 10 days to file a response. The complaint must have been prompted by his helping his attorney friend.

McTavish called a number on the letter to inquire about what licensing might be needed to collect a fee in assisting buyers and sellers in a merger or acquisition. The short answer was he needed to be a licensed stockbroker to accept a fee for a stock deal and a real estate license to accept a fee for the sale of real estate or goodwill. Of course, he wasn't licensed as either. But the good news was he had not accepted a fee for the two or three hours of assistance he had provided for the attorney. A fine, a penalty, or jail time had been avoided by being generous.

***

A few weeks later, McTavish decided to make some revisions in the investment make-up of his pension fund, and a visit to his stockbroker was in order. Leonard Sanderson was not only a trusted stockbroker but also a long-time friend, and they met over lunch. After deciding a few portfolio changes, Sanderson changed the subject.

"For a long time, I've wanted to open my own shop. I have a very nice book of business and could get significantly more of the local bank trust company's business if I had my own shop."

"What's stopping you?"

"A stock brokerage firm needs two licensed principals: Registered

YOU JUST CAN'T MAKE THIS STUFF UP...

or operational and Financial. I could pass the test and qualify for a Registered Principal, but I need someone who could pass the test for and serve as a Financial Principal." At that point Sanderson looked McTavish knowingly and asked, "Do you know anyone?"

McTavish mind went back to the requirements for accepting fees for assisting a merger or acquisition. You needed to be licensed as either a stockbroker or a real estate agent. After a moment of reflection, his answer changed his life.

"I think I do." And the security broker/dealer firm of Sanderson and McTavish was conceptually born.

CHAPTER FIVE

EARLY IN 1990

*"During a pending business acquisition, allowing
the buyer and the seller to be in the same room
without intermediaries can have unintended and
disappointing consequences."* **–Jay M. Bylsma**

With 16 employees in the shop and $1,800,000 in sales, Harry's connections and assiduously living up to the CORE Machining name (Customer Oriented Relationships Exemplified), CORE had averaged a nearly 20% annual growth rate. At an average net income of 12.5%, both CORE and Harry were debt free. In addition, Harry had diligently contributed to the 401k program he had in place at CORE, and while money doesn't buy happiness, a quarter of a million in a retirement account added to the worth of his business bought a pile of peace of mind.

But there were customers, good customers, who had metal-working problems that Harry couldn't help them with, and that led to some discomfort. He felt the need to expand by adding more services to his capabilities. Electrical Discharge Machining, or EDM as it was commonly called, offered the ability to cut intricate shapes in heavy gauge metal with a high degree of accuracy. An electrical spark is created between an electrode and the workpiece, creating temperatures in excess of 14,000 degrees Fahrenheit, which can melt almost anything.

He called an acquaintance, David McTavish, a business intermediary, or broker, who specialized in small to medium-size businesses and indicated his interest in exploring the possibility of acquiring a shop that specialized in EDM.

McTavish returned the call a few weeks later and indicated there was a small EDM shop in a resort city on Lake Michigan about 12 miles away that the owner was considering selling. Harry agreed to meet the McTavish at the place of business the following Tuesday. McTavish faxed the appropriate non-disclosure agreements and, on receiving them signed, followed up with the company's tax returns and financial statements for the past five years. $800,000 in net sales projected for the current year would be a nice addition to his top line and $100, 000 in net income would fit nicely on his bottom line. But what attracted Harry more was that the customer list included only two of Harry's current customers. The 30 or so other customers provided fertile ground to plow for CORE's machining business.

The location and the physical plant were not the best, but the equipment was in excellent condition, and the range of its capabilities was just what Harry thought he needed. The owner was cordial, and Harry found him to be candid in his answers. His reason for selling was that he had health issues that could be alleviated by living in a less humid and warmer climate. The asking price of $750,000 was reasonable.

In the parking lot after saying good-bye to the owner, Harry told the McTavish this was what he was looking for, and he would instruct his attorney to draw up a Letter of Intent to purchase the business. When he got back to CORE, he phoned Lisa and told her he had found an EDM shop to buy.

That night was spent discussing how this purchase could work. He would need to rent another bay or two in the loft he was occupying. The owner's salary would not be needed and would more than pay for the additional rent. Besides offering his current customers the possibility of EDM, the EDM shop's customer list contained thirty customers who might be persuaded to give CORE some of their machining needs.

The night ended with Lisa as excited about the prospects of this new venture as Harry. Harry had some additional questions for the seller and wanted to see the place again, and Lisa wanted to see what Harry was so excited about for herself.

A call to McTavish arranged the visit for the following Saturday. "My wife Lisa is my partner, and I want her to see the business, and I have some additional questions of the owner," Harry explained.

A meeting was set up for the following Saturday afternoon. The owner was gracious and forthright as he answered Harry's additional questions and took great pains to explain the concept of Electrical Discharge Machining to Lisa, showing her parts that had been made on his equipment that could only be done by this process. The meeting concluded by Harry saying to the owner, "You have been most generous with your time on a Saturday afternoon and I see it's 5:30. We must say good-bye and thank you for your opening the shop on Saturday to accommodate us. One more thing before we go, where would you recommend we have dinner in your town?"

"Oh dear, I'm afraid there's no place that would accommodate you without reservations, this being a Saturday night in the summer in a resort town. But as it happens, my wife and I have reservations at the Blue Heron for 6:30 tonight. It's the best place in town and I'd be honored if you would join us. What do you say?"

Harry didn't read the "NO, NO, NO" in the eyes of McTavish. All he saw was the "YES" in Lisa's eyes.

"That's very gracious of you. We would love to join you," was Harry's reply.

***

David McTavish's phone rang at seven o'clock. It was Harry.

"I'm sorry to say the deal is off."

"How come? What happened?"

"It appears all the graciousness in that couple resides in him. His wife began what can only be called "cat fighting" while we were waiting for a table, and it continued when we seated. She left the table in a huff before the drinks were finished and we could order. He was very apologetic. Apparently, she doesn't want him to sell, at least not to us. I'm sorry. Please keep looking for an EDM shop for me to buy."

CHAPTER SIX

LATER IN 1990

"You can dictate the price or dictate the terms, but you don't get to dictate both." –**Randy Rua**

When Harry picked up the ringing phone, James Bateman, Jr. was the last person he expected to hear. Jamie (as he liked to be called) came right to the point. Could they have a private dinner at Jamie's country club, sometime soon, say next Saturday night?

Harry recalled the last time he had dinner at the country club was Jim Bateman's retirement party. And he remembered that hadn't turned out so well for him. But he thought he knew what this meeting was going to be about. Jamie's shop had remained relatively stagnant, certainly not growing like CORE, and the reason for that was largely CORE. Jamie was looking for a buyer and Harry was the most likely candidate. Harry could only guess how much crow Jamie had to swallow to dial his number.

Harry still had the same Jerry Garcia tie he had worn to Jim Bateman, Sr.'s retirement party, and he decided it would be appropriately ironic to wear it again. Jamie's wine glass was almost empty when Harry arrived at a table in the corner of the country club's elegant dining room.

After some stiff formalities, Jamie came right to the point. "I've given the business my father left me my best efforts. But I underestimated how stiff the competition would become," he said with a wry smile. "My wife's health is declining, and she never liked Michigan—she's a California girl and is bugging me to hang up this shingle and move her to San Francisco where her family is. So, Dyno is for sale and you are the most likely buyer for obvious reasons."

Harry wasn't sure what the obvious reasons were, but he held his questions as a waiter approached. Jamie recommended the braised beef short ribs. Harry ordered the scallops, and when they were alone again, Jamie continued. "Most of the really good machinists and machine operators are still at Dyno, and you know how hard it is to find skill in this day and age when it seems everyone thinks the only way to the American dream is in incur four years of college debt. And you would recognize most of the customers I've been able to keep . . ."

As Jamie went through what appeared to be a rehearsed sales pitch, Harry's mind was racing. Good help is very hard to get, and Dyno had some excellent machinists. Jamie had priced his bids with very little margin, forcing Harry to be more competitive than he wished to be, and the new building he had just completed and moved into had anticipated growth. Not to mention what a coup it would be finally to acquire the company he had hoped and planned to own some ten or more years ago, so he wouldn't, at least not out loud. And so, the negotiation began.

Harry: "Jamie, I'm flattered you would think of me first. Unfortunately, I just made a significant financial commitment in constructing my own building, and this opportunity might be coming at an inopportune time for me."

Jamie: "I've driven past the place. You did a nice job on it. I like the way you made a revetment pond to handle your run-off. Very nice. If you are saying this may be more than you are prepared to undertake financially at the moment, I would be willing to look at terms."

Harry: "I'm saying any businessman would be a fool not to at least look into any opportunity that comes along. But the timing may not be the best for me at the moment. But, I'm willing to see what you have and listen to what you want for it."

Jamie: "I haven't come down hard on a price as yet. I have a fraternity brother who is in the merger and acquisition business. I've sent him my information, and he hasn't gotten back to me yet. I'm afraid he's into nine-figure deals and may not have to time to do me this favor."

Harry: "How many people do you have on the floor?"

Jamie: "Twelve at the moment. The economic downturn in the late '80s did me no favors."

Harry: "Are you willing to share more information informally?"

Jamie: "Funny you should ask. I just happen to have a Confidentially Agreement with me. If you're interested and willing to sign it, I'll tell you whatever you want to know, including sending you my recent financial statements."

Harry: "Let's see what you want me to sign."

It was a standard non-disclosure agreement, and Harry signed it with the notation, "for myself and the officers of CORE Machining, Inc."

Jamie: "If I may ask, who are the officers of your company?"

Harry: "My controller and my wife. What are you looking for, stock deal or asset purchase?"

Jamie: "I'm told by my accountant that a stock deal would have more favorable tax consequences, but depending on the structure of the deal, I could be flexible."

Harry: "Well, I have to say my curiosity is piqued. I'm interested enough to give it a look. If you would be willing to send me your current Statement of Financial Position, Income Statement, and the past five years tax returns, I'll look it over and be back to you soon, say within the week, with an indication of my interest. Fair enough?"

Jamie: "Fair enough."

The scallops were outstanding.

***

On receiving the information, Harry met with his business broker, David McTavish. The tax returns showed only modest growth over the past five years, the Statement of Financial Position showed $90,000 in long term debt. The Income Statement showed $1,140,000 in annual sales and a cash flow of $228,000.

"Interesting," mused McTavish, "How did he present himself at your meeting?"

"He left me with the clear impression he needs or wants desperately to sell," Harry replied. "First of all, he had to eat a lot of crow to call me, and he had his non-disclosure agreement at the ready. It may be that his wife hates Michigan, but I rather suspect a stagnant machining business lacks the kind of luster you might wish to talk about at Harvard Business School class reunions.

"I think he thought with his education, he could take this business over and within a few years be ready for an IPO. He found out that machining is a commodity and is done in job shops, of which there are dozens within shouting distance of those with whom you will be competing. I think he's had enough. His father passed away a year ago, and he may have held on even this long to please Jim senior."

"How strong is your interest to buy this, will it fit into your plans, and can you assimilate it?" David asked.

"I can easily assimilate it. It would eliminate a competitor who is always low-balling his bids. That shows in that he is only making $90K a year per operator while I'm $110K per operator. I'm just afraid he might be reasonable on the terms but will over-value the business. You know, the 3M valuation method: 'Make Me a Millionaire.'"

"Well, the valuation is not complicated. He has no proprietary products, he does not show above-industry average growth, his revenue per operator is less than what it should be (compared to yours), so the value is a range of between three point five to four times his $280,000 in cash flow. The value is between $798,000 and $912,000 debt free, say between $800,000 and $900,000. Will he sell for less than a million?"

"There's only one way to find out."

Harry's lawyer drew up the LOI (Letter of Intent) at $800,000 in cash, or $900,000 with $450,000 down and $100,000 in a Covenant Not to Compete and $350,000 to be paid over a five-year period at 8% interest.

James Bateman, Jr. did indeed have a different opinion of the value of Dyno, actually more than the "3M Business Valuation Method" Harry mentioned to McTavish. And he turned down Harry's offer summarily. But apparently his wife's desire to move to San Francisco trumped whatever valuation methodology Jamie was using. Six months later, negotiations resumed, and Dyno was acquired by CORE for $750,000 in cash and a $100,000 Covenant Not to Compete to be paid over a three-year period.

Harry was pleased, and so was his banker. Not so much the Harvard Business School grad. Not incidentally, he thought Lisa's smile at the closing of the sale was a bit too smug. Who did she think she was? After all, she had "Junior College" written all over her.

CHAPTER SEVEN

SOON AFTER THE DYNO ACQUISITION

"You can't look at a service business with a manufacture's eyes, or your vice will verse you." -Jay M. Bylsma

Lisa Harrington had kept the books for CORE Machining, Inc. for the first seven years of its existence, until they outgrew their accounting package—QuickBooks—and a real-life accountant was hired. She remained the Corporate Secretary and together, she and Harry made most of the significant decisions.

When the last of her children left for college, she enrolled in business courses at the local college and found she had an interest in marketing. She was the one who insisted on CORE having a website: "It's the wave of the future, Harry." And it was.

She insisted on a monthly postcard mailing to all their present and former customers and every company she could think of in West Michigan that could possibly use the services of a machine shop. "Not only to keep our name in front of our customers, but sooner or later this will mean new business, Harry." And it did. Sooner.

Over dinner one night, she popped the question. Her question: "Harry, I'd like us to find a business for me, something I can have and hold like you have CORE."

Harry was almost speechless. "Sweetheart, are you serious?"

"Yes, I'm serious. I've been thinking about it for a while. Do you suppose David, the intermediary we used when we bought Dyno, would help us?"

Harry knew it would be futile to dissuade her, but he tried. "How about we make you VP of Marketing at CORE?"

"Harry, I don't want a title, I want a challenge, something of my own. Something where I can put my education to use, limited as it is."

***

It happened that David McTavish had been contacted about a year prior by the owner of a service business who had made some general inquiries about when a good time was to sell a business and what he could expect to get for a service business like his. David had met with him and gone over the things an owner should do to prepare his business for the optimum outcome should he sell. That is, prepare an exit plan so that you are in control of when and how you exit, you are ready when an opportunity presents itself, you maximize what you put in your pocket, you beat the very high-percentage failure rate, you communicate your intentions to your family and your employees, and so forth.

In addition, there were conversations about how to enhance the value of the business and how the business would be valued. It was apparent the owner had some housekeeping to do to get ready for a sale should an opportunity arise. David had kept the contact information, and he called this owner to see if he was ready to entertain the possibility of selling.

"I was just thinking of calling you. Something has come up—it's a partnership opportunity in my former line of work that I would like to take advantage of. Only things that are holding me back are cash and this business. Selling it would solve both."

"Remind me again what it is you do," replied David.

"We repair and rebuild automatic electrostatic industrial paint guns."

David mused, "That doesn't sound very sexy."

"We make 25% before taxes. That should be sexy enough for anyone."

***

A tour was arranged for the following Friday after the company's employees had gone home. Visually, sexy it wasn't. The process of scraping and baking off months of accumulated dried paint, repairing, and reassembling the units was a dirty process. There were several carts of units completely disassembled and waiting for repair. The owner was walking them through the process. "We do about thirty of these a month with three employees, up from twenty a month and two employees last year. With the growth we see coming in the door, I expect we will be in the vicinity of forty a month next year."

"To what do you attribute your growth?"

"Nearest competition is located Cincinnati and is a subsidiary of a German company. Because of their overhead, they charge about 15% more than we do. Add the cost of round-trip shipping, and we have about a 25% cost advantage, not to mention a quicker turn-around time. Plus, we offer an exchange program where we will loan you a spray gun—for a fee—until yours can be repaired."

"How do you do your marketing?"

"I have a list of the 250 industrial painters in the Midwest. I try to call one Head of Maintenance a week. We are thinking of getting a website, but so far we've been too busy to do anything about that."

In the parking lot, Harry, Lisa, and David discussed what they had seen.

Lisa: "It's dirty, messy, unkempt, and not very orderly."

Harry: "There's hardly any equipment to buy—a furnace, some hand tools. He does have good documentation on the repair manuals of a lot of different guns. Seems it would be easy to get up to speed on how to repair them."

David: "It appears to be an untapped market. Is this something you think you would enjoy marketing, Lisa?"

Lisa: "Like I said before, it's not very sexy. How does one dress to call on a company's Head of Maintenance?"

David: "I've asked for his financial statements. You think about whether this is a business you may have an interest in, and after we get the financials, let's meet again."

***

Later that week, they met in David's office. "As I'm sure you've seen from the financials, this is a lucrative business. From his cash flow at current capitalization rates, the business would be valued at $1.2 million. But there is a wrinkle. I received a fax from the owner this morning. A new customer he's been working on gave him a trial order of one gun a week over a month. If it successful, it could amount to that volume over the next year and beyond. He's suggesting that if we choose to make an offer, it should include the impact of this new customer."

Harry's wrinkled brow belied some disbelief. "I'm aware that the value of a business is the discounted present value of future earnings, but what if this so-called 'new business' doesn't pan out? Can one make an offer contingent on the realization of this new business?"

Lisa was more direct. "$1.2 million? For what, a furnace and some inventory carts? There can't be a quarter of a million dollars' worth of equipment!"

"This is a service business. It has a $300,000 annual cash flow on $1.2 million in sales without any equipment to speak of. It's like an accounting practice, which doesn't have much in the way of hard assets, either. You are accustomed to a manufacturing environment where you are equipment-rich and do well to have a $125,000 cash flow on $1.2 million in sales."

After looking a Lisa and getting only a shoulder shrug, Harry suggested David present a verbal offer of $1,000,000 in cash. "If he is really in need of some quick cash, this might tempt him."

***

The owner shook his head at $1,000,000. "I think it's only fair some consideration be made for the impending new business. It doesn't have to be up front, but something—a commission or a share of the profits if and when it comes."

***

After reporting the refusal to Harry and Lisa, David drew up several proposals for their consideration. They contained various

JAY M. BYLSMA AND RANDY RUA

options with less cash up front but with the possibility of more than $1.2 million should the new business be realized. After the Harringtons considered these possibilities, David received their phone call. "We're willing to pay 1 million in cash, but nothing more. For various reasons, this just doesn't feel right to Lisa, and I'm not willing to go ahead without her complete buy-in. It's going to be 1 million, take it or leave it."

He left it.

***

David chanced to run into the owner two years later at a business leadership conference and, after exchanging pleasantries, asked the man how he was doing. It was a very satisfying smile on the owner's face that preceded the comment—no, it was more like an announcement—that sales were $3.5 million and margins had improved. David didn't think the Rolex the owner was wearing was a knock-off.

44

CHAPTER EIGHT

SEVERAL MONTHS LATER

"If you are going to 'set out a fleece,' you are setting yourself up to get fleeced, or (to say it another way), you don't need to ask you employees if you should sell; the probability of their answer can be predicted with a 99% confidence level." –Jay M. Bylsma

Background Note: *The world's first heart transplantation was performed by Christiaan Barnard in South Africa in December 1967. Dr. Norman Shumway and his surgical team at the Stanford University Medical Center performed the first successful adult human heart transplant in the United States on January 6, 1968*.*

D avid McTavish was always pleased to take a call from a college classmate, George Rogers. Rogers was the president of a large religious charitable foundation located in Chicago and had a problem. He had a wealthy, generous donor who wished

---

* https://med.stanford.edu/news/all-news/2006/02/norman-shum-way-heart-transplantation-pioneer-dies-at-83.html

to take advantage of the foundation's free estate planning in exchange for a bequest to the foundation.

"Sven Andersen is widowed and has no heirs and has a medical instrument business in Redwood City, California. He is past the age where he should be the president of any business and wishes to donate the business to the foundation. We are not in the business of running a medical instrument business, either, and Mr. Andersen has agreed to entertain selling. Would you be willing to go out to California, meet with Mr. Andersen, determine what his business is worth, and assess whether it can be marketed? It might be problematic as the business has a very small market and little or no assets. And if it is sellable, I'd like you to represent Mr. Andersen in the sale."

"Do you have any idea of the size of this business?"

"I've been out to see him. He operates it out of a hole-in-the-fence place with two employees. However, from the size of some of his annual contributions to the foundation, it must be very profitable."

"Very profitable" was enough to pique David's interest, and he checked on possible flights.

On arriving in San Francisco, David rented a car but had some difficulty in finding Andersen Medical Equipment, Inc. in Redwood City as the address indicated a shabby building with a front no bigger than a two-stall garage at the head of an ally. There was no signage, and it was in a neglected residential area. Roger's description of a hole-in-the-fence was not overstated. The front door was locked, but on his knock the door was opened by a stooped and wizened man, apparently in his late 70s or 80s, who eyed David suspiciously.

"Mr. Andersen, my name is David McTavish. I was sent by George Rogers from the Saint Gregory Foundation. I believe he indicated you would be expecting me?"

Without a word, Mr. Andersen opened the door and stepped aside, an apparent indication David was welcome to enter.

"I vas to haf mine coffee break, vill you shoin me?" Without waiting for David to reply, he turned into a very small office that had a hotplate and a coffee pot on a two-drawer filing cabinet. Sven Andersen poured two cups and spooned two sugars in each, handed one to David, took a seat in an old swivel desk chair, and pointed to a folding chair for David.

"Mr. Andersen, I—"

"Ef ve are to do en business, you vill call me Sven, yah?"

"Okay, Sven, please call me David. What is that you do here?

Andersen began at the beginning. He worked at the Stanford University Medical Center, maintaining the plant and its equipment. When Dr. Shumway began doing heart transplants, some were successful, and some patients rejected the transplanted organ. The problem was there was no way to tell if the transplanted heart was being rejected until it was too late to save the patient. Shumway needed a way to biopsy the heart on a regular basis after surgery to foresee the possibility of rejection so the patient's medication could be changed in time to save the heart. Could Sven create an instrument that would enter the femoral artery and take a biopsy of the heart tissue—an "endometrial biopsy"?

"Yah, I try," was Sven's reply. But he made Dr. Shumway promise it would be tried on a dog before it was to be used on a human as Sven didn't want his idea to be the cause of someone's death should it not work.

Sven's idea was to take a medical clamp and attach it to a wire encapsulated in a hollow cable that was small enough and long enough to reach from the entry site in the leg to the heart and attach a very small cupped cutter. Opening and closing the clamp would open and close the cutter, which would take a tissue sample from the transplanted heart to be withdrawn and tested for rejection.

The next day he showed his sample to the doctor, who bypassed

47

the experiment on a dog and successfully biopsied a patient's heart. "Sven, you have no idea how important this instrument is. It will make heart transplants a viable clinical treatment to the degree it was not possible before."

Word got around in the medical community, and the demand for Sven's instrument was such that he left the employ of the Medical Center and formed Andersen Medical Equipment, Inc. and could hardly make the instruments fast enough to satisfy the demand for both new instruments and reconditioned ones that had been previously sold and needed the "nippers" to be sharpened. A new instrument sold for $700, and Sven charged $200 to recondition used ones.

During a tour through the small shop, David quickly saw why Mr. Andersen's donations to the Saint Gregory Foundation could be sizable. The cost of the instrument could be no more than $45, and he was selling it for $700 as fast as he could make them.

Back in the small office, the conversation became earnest. "In order to help you, Sven, I will need to see your financial statements. Or I could use your last year's federal income tax return."

"Ant vhat vould det tell you?"

"What you could expect to sell your business for."

David could see Mr. Andersen was reluctant to divulge this most sacred of information. But after an uncomfortable moment or two, he opened the small file cabinet and handed David a manila folder. The first page of the tax return showed David almost everything he needed to know. $630,000 in pre-tax profit on $1,050,000 in sales.

***

The first person to whom David thought to show the business was a member of his Lodge who had a falling out as the Vice

President of Sales of a large medical equipment company and was recently unemployed. He accompanied David on a trip to Redwood City to visit Mr. Anderson and see the business that made what he considered unconscionable profits (but which he confessed wouldn't bother his conscience). On the return flight, he decided to make an offer but indicated he didn't have the resources to make a cash offer. However, he had close relationship with one of the managers of a local venture capital fund called Questing. He would arrange to meet with them next week and would have an answer by the following Friday.

David knew the local inventor who had become very wealthy on his invention and had put $300,000,000 into this venture capital company. Questing was always looking for just this kind of business in which to invest. This, plus this buyer's relationship with the manager of the fund, would most certainly be the source of capital he needed.

Certainty turned into disappointment, however, when the manager turned the opportunity down because . . . wait for it . . . the opportunity only had one product. Oh, the irony. The fortune that was made with one product turned this opportunity down because it only had one product.

Two more trips with interested buyers were unsuccessful for various reasons.

The fourth visitor was the president of a small medical device company that specialized in inexpensive disposable instruments (therefore eliminating the need to sterilize reusable instruments). It was also being recognized for its leadership in making instruments for the new medical technique of non-invasive surgery. This buyer saw more possibilities for the Andersen instrument than endometrial biopsies and agreed to the $2.5-million price.

David flew out again to present the offer to Mr. Andersen in the form of a Letter of Intent to Buy. They discussed at length the qualifications of the buyer, the salient fact to Andersen that he was a fine Christian man as evidenced by his record of also donating to the Saint Gregory Foundation, that the biopsy instrument would be a fine addition to their existing line of medical devices, and, importantly, how much good the Saint Gregory Foundation could do with the money to be generated by the sale. David got Andersen's signature on the Letter of Intent to Buy.

The buyer instructed his attorney to prepare the necessary sales documents, and arrangements were made for the buyer and his attorney, along with David, to go to California for the closing on the following Wednesday. On Monday evening, David was finishing supper when the home phone rang. "Would you accept a person-to-person call from Redwood City, California?"

"Ya, David. Sven here. I call to say I do not sell my business."

"Sven, what happened? What changed your mind?"

"I am like Gideon in dah Bible. I set out un fleece und dah fleece say I do not sell."

"And what was the fleece you set out, Sven, if I may ask?"

"I asked God vot He vant me to do. He tell me ask my two employees if day vant me to sell or keep dah business. Dey tell me not to sell."

It wasn't just the $105,000 in expected fees that took wing on that phone call, but the almost $10,000 in travel expenses that were spent in vain.

***

Two years later, David receive a phone call from George Rogers from the foundation. "I called to tell you I received news that Sven Andersen passed away. As I am the executor of his will, I thought you would be interested to learn that another medical instrument company came up with a plastic disposable endometrial biopsy device and took over the market. In addition, needle biopsies have been introduced into the mix to biopsy the other side of the heart to further reduce the demand for his instrument. He had to lay off his two employees. Andersen's was left with the business of only refurbishing instruments he had sold, for which he charged more than the disposable instruments cost. Soon enough the whole world was using the disposable instruments and needle biopsies. The heart transplant world is no longer centered on his little shop. His pastor told me he died a bitter man. Not to mention what the foundation could have done with $2.5 million. I guess I did just mention that, didn't I?"

"As it turns out," David mused, "the ones he used as his fleece were the cause of him being fleeced."

Coincidence on top of irony.

CHAPTER NINE

Many large companies outsource some of their HR (Human Resources) functions to third-party administrators. For example, Paychex will handle all timekeeping and payroll functions. Others administer health insurance programs. Administrative Professionals, LLC. (Ad Pro) was one such company that handled the day-to-day administration of the health insurance benefit of employees for several very large companies. They answered employees' questions, processed claims, administered pre-employment physicals, etc.

Megan Sutter was the company's founder and sole owner, having worked for a similar large firm in Chicago before returning to her hometown in Western Michigan to start Ad Pro. In 16 years, the firm had grown to serve several large clients, employ 125 associates, and make over a million dollars in income before executive bonuses and income tax. Sutter had grown to own a million-dollar mansion on the shores of Lake Michigan. She also had acquired three addictions: her grandchildren, the million-dollar home on Lake Michigan, and cigarettes. So, while she could be found in her office at 6:00 on Monday morning, she had her feet in the sand on the shore by noon on Thursday watching a grandchild or two make sand castles.

Kenneth Dekker was a VP-Sales at Ad Pro. He was an early hire—fresh out of the local junior college with an associate degree in marketing and had worked his way up the ladder while getting his bachelor's degree nights and weekends. Having been responsible for securing five of the seven large clients Ad Pro served, he felt justifiably responsible for a large measure of the company's success and justifiably miffed (in his mind, at least) that the more successful Ad Pro became, the less Megan Sutter seemed to be around. There was the three-and-a-half-day work week, out-of-town conferences aplenty, and more vacation time than anyone else was entitled to take. And in her absence, all the questions and decisions fell to him.

Dekker went to the office of Ad Pro's VP of Finance and closed the door. "What would you think of getting the officers together to form a group to buy Megan out?"

"Tell me you're not serious!"

"I'm dead serious. As a group, we run the place anyway, why shouldn't we own it and share more in the profits?"

"Frankly, I've entertained a thought or two about it, but this is a sales and service organization, and I'm an introvert. I would have to drag you and the others along with me and I thought that would only happen, with you in particular, kicking and screaming."

Dekker was pleased with that reply and he asked, "What is the business worth?"

"Off the top of my head, 5 million. I hope you can come up with most of that. I can't."

"Neither can I, but with the company's track record, we should be able to get most of it financed, and I would hope Sutter has enough confidence in our future to hold some paper."

YOU JUST CAN'T MAKE THIS STUFF UP...

"Getting bank financing will be difficult. We have no assets for them to collateralize. This is a service company. We don't have any assets except office furniture and equipment for them hold as security for a loan."

Dekker was not expecting that response and paused for a moment. Then, "So how does one go about trying to buy a business?"

"You start with someone who's experienced in this sort of thing—an intermediary or broker. I know of one in town. His name is David Mc-something-or-other. I'll look him up and get his particulars to you."

***

Dekker's visit with David McTavish was productive but not altogether satisfactory. The business was indeed worth $5 million, and the present officers were a good choice for a buyer. The questions were, would Sutter sell, and how should she be approached? McTavish's advice was that Dekker approach her himself because, if McTavish approached her, it could be construed as Dekker going behind her back.

Dekker had gone to his bank and the VP of Finance was correct: the bank would not finance much of the deal. They would only lend up to $2 million, and that only with the personal guarantees of the officers and their wives, and any paper carried by Sutter would have to be subordinate to the bank. In addition, the total of cash the officers were able to contribute was $750,000 which would require Sutter to carry $2.25 million in notes. On the other hand, $5 million at 6% interest should provide for a comfortable lifestyle—with careful budgeting. And one could put one's feet in the sand every day.

***

The meeting with Megan Sutter was congenial enough. Dekker explained he was representing most of the officers in the offer to buy her out. It was their intent to continue to grow the business she had started. She could maintain an office, retain her seat on the board of directors, come and go as she pleased, and would continue to be an employee for health insurance benefits. The price would be $5 million with $2,750,000 down and $2,250,000 in a note to her at 8% interest with monthly payments of principal and interest over seven years.

In the end, it was the bank's requirement that Sutter's note be subordinated to their note, as well as the size of the note, that caused her to reject the offer.

The business continued as usual, and so did Sutter.

CHAPTER TEN

SEVERAL MONTHS LATER

"One man's treasure is another man's junk." –Randy Rua

Rudder Machine, Inc. was a small machine shop that James Harrington (Harry) had heard of but with whom he rarely competed. His one contact had been when a machinist answered a "Help Wanted - Machinist" ad Harry had placed in the local paper. With high schools sending 80% of their students off to college in search of the good life, qualified machinists were getting harder and harder to find. So, when a machinist with 15 years of experience answered the ad, it seemed too good to be true. And it was. When Harry checked with Rudder Machine, his most recent employer, he learned the applicant was dismissed for chronic absence due to alcoholism.

"Rudder is a specialty machine shop with some unusual capabilities. It satisfies a niche that may well fit in with what you do. You should at least take a look at it. The asking price is $2.5 million, and the appraised value of the equipment is $2 million." It was David McTavish on the phone.

Harry had long ago learned that you had to kiss a lot of toads before you find a handsome prince, and while he thought Rudder Machine was a toad, you never knew. So, he agreed to meet at the facility the following day for a "look see." But he was skeptical. Princes are usually not for sale for the appraised value of the equipment. This would probably be a toad.

Rudder Machine was located in an older building but was well maintained, as were the grounds. After introductions, Harry was given an equipment appraisal done by Fredericksen, an auction house with a good reputation for fair and accurate appraisals. The equipment was what one might expect to find in a machine shop. Some were new, most were old, some were ancient. However, nearly every piece was outfitted with an extraneous device ("gadget" came to Harry's mind) to perform some secondary operation. Most, if not all, of these devices were designed and made in-house by Horace Rudder himself, and some were very clever operations.

"This one is a specialty piece to insert ball bearings into this nylon roller to be used in drawer slides for the furniture industry. This one is designed to automatically encapsulate an O-ring seal onto this fitting before the end is expanded and then chamfered," Rudder explained proudly as they went from machine to machine.

In the parking lot after the tour, McTavish asked Harry what he thought.

"Interesting operation, and there are some operations I could incorporate into CORE. But something is troublesome. I have this appraisal from Fredericksen, which indicated $2 million, but I didn't see $2 million worth of equipment. He has some nice pieces, and he has a lot of gimcracks installed to perform his specialty operation, but I don't see $2 million."

"I've always found Fredericksen to be a reputable appraiser," was McTavish's reply. "What do you think the equipment is worth?"

"Maybe a touch more than a million, but not much more. Certainly not two million."

"You serious?"

"Dead serious. This operations piques my interest, but besides the issue with the valuation, I would need to find someone with the inventive skills Rudder has to even maintain all his handmade secondary operations. Secondary operations are not my forte, but I've been thinking about it, and this could be my entree into this part of machining."

"So, what should I tell Mr. Rudder?"

"Tell him he has piqued my interest and I'd like some time to look over this appraisal. I'll get back to you in a day or two."

***

Harry's controller poured over the financial statements while Harry reviewed the Fredericksen appraisal. Piece by piece, everything appeared to be inflated.

"Take this device he has for inserting ball bearings into the nylon roller. The appraised value is $75,000. There's not $25,000 worth of parts in it. And the next piece, that press is old, and the cut-off device attached to it is clever, but that cut-off device doesn't make the press worth $50,000." And so, it went.

As far as the financial statements were concerned, the controller advised Harry that he could value the $175,000 in net income and $200,000 in interest and depreciation at no more than $1.5 million, versus the $2.5-million asking price.

"David. Harry here. Regarding Rudder Machine, I have an interest, but I have some serious reservations about the equipment appraisal at $2 million. I've looked it over quite carefully, and I don't see much more than 1 million. So, here's my thinking. I'll pay for a second appraisal. We'll see where that comes in and go from there."

***

The second appraisal came in at $1.2 million, and the explanation for the discrepancy was that Rudder had convinced Fredericksen that the secondary operations increased the value of the underlying equipment. And while the secondary operations had value of their own, it was not $800,000.

Harry called McTavish with the news. "So, I continue to have an interest but not at $2.5 million. I'm afraid Rudder has 2.5 million in his head and will not like to hear $1.5 million or anything less than $2 million. But at 2.5 million, I'm not interested. I don't have $1.5 million lying around and will have to finance the purchase, and the bank is going to insist on their own appraisers, who won't find $2 million worth of equipment, either."

Harry was right, Rudder wouldn't budge on his $2.5-million asking price. McTavish was unable to find another buyer for the business, and eventually the business was taken off the market. Then the recession hit, and Rudder was unable to satisfy the bank's loan requirements. The bank foreclosed on the loan and the equipment, which was liquidated at auction. Rudder's treasures went for a total of $700,000.

Harry didn't attend the auction.

CHAPTER ELEVEN

SOMETIME IN 1995

"Your banker is not going to ask God if the loan should be granted. You'll need the right answers to all his or her questions." –Jay M. Bylsma

HiQual Steel Products was one of Harry's best customers; their relationship went back to Harry's Dyno days. So, calls from Jeff Farmer, HiQual's president, were not uncommon—until this one. Farmer was asking for a breakfast meeting. HiQual had bid on a very large contract to furnish steel structural parts and was successful, only to find out that its roll form supplier was declaring bankruptcy. The roll formed parts required some sophisticated machining, for which Harry had been the successful bidder.

Over pancakes, Farmer proposed that Harry become HiQual's source for roll forming. The previous supplier had equipment to be liquidated and employees who were technically qualified and looking for a job. Harry had the space. Farmer promised at least a half a million in annual sales, and there would be other customers for the bankrupt firm's book of business.

Farmer arranged for Harry and a member of his newly formed board of directors, Peter Lantinga, to tour the closed-down facility. The reason for the bankruptcy was readily apparent—the debt on too much very expensive equipment couldn't be supported in the 1990 economic downturn. The specter of all this equipment sitting silently was a sickening sight.

Harry and Farmer decided on the pieces Harry would need to set CORE up as a quality roll form operation. Negotiations with the Clerk of the Bankruptcy Court did not go well. He wanted Harry to buy all-or-nothing and not cherry-pick only what he needed. But due to some pressing secured creditors who wanted their cash sooner rather than later and the very soft market for used equipment, he relented, and Harry bought the pieces he needed for $900,000 C.O.D., pending approval from the CORE Board of Directors.

One of the five board members was the head of the commercial loan department at the City First Bank where Harry had done his banking since he started CORE. "With your record with the bank, assuming you are willing to collateralize the equipment, there will be no trouble extending you a competitive term loan." The motion to purchase the equipment with the help of the term loan passed, and Harry confirmed the purchase with the Bankruptcy Court.

The next week, on Wednesday morning, Harry received notification the equipment would be delivered on Friday, and he was reminded by the trucking company the delivery would be C.O.D.— Certified Funds. Harry called the loan officer to indicate the loan would have to be processed and a certified check ready by Friday.

The loan officer was not forthright. "Yes, well . . . ah, we'll have it ready, but my father would like to talk to you about this financing."

His father was the president of the bank.

"Okay, when?"

"How about two o'clock this afternoon?"

"I'll be there." Strange. It's a big loan, but why would the bank president involve himself?

***

Harry's usual lunch hangout was the counter at PW's Grill, where he chanced to run into Peter Lantinga. "Any word on when the equipment's coming?"

"Yes, it will arrive on Friday. By the way, when I called the loan officer to be sure the financing is set, he told me I need to have a conversation with his father. You are on the board of the bank—what do you suppose that's all about?"

"When are you meeting?" Lantinga wore concern on his face.

"This afternoon at two o'clock."

"Don't go to that meeting alone. Let me come with you!" And Peter was adamant.

***

The president's office was a huge room on the second floor above and the size of the lobby of the bank, and his desk was on a raised platform. The chairs they were invited to sit in were not. Harry had to raise his head to see the president, who had to peer over his nose to see Harry. The nursery rhyme "The King is in his counting house, counting out his money" came to mind.

"Peter, nice to see you, but what are you doing here?"

"I'm on the CORE Board of Directors, and I came to hear what you have to say about this loan."

"Yes, very well, the bank is prepared to assist you in this purchase. We've been watching your progress with great interest. But we feel your balance sheet would look a lot better with some additional equity instead of a loan of this magnitude, in the event additional borrowing may become necessary, what with your growth and all. In addition, as you know, Peter, my son Anthony is graduating from Amherst with his degree in economics, which we feel is just the sort of expertise your growing business needs—"

Peter cut the president short. "Thank you very much. We'll take your offer under advisement. Come on Harry, let's go."

It took Harry a moment to realize the meeting was over. Peter was out of his chair and starting to leave.

When they hit the street, Harry blurted out, "What just happened in there?"

"That family and their country club cronies own half the big businesses in town, and this is just how they acquire them. The bank gets you in a spot where you need the money and have no choice but to accept their terms. And their terms are to eventually own you. They've done it time and time again, but they're not going to get away with it this time. We're going across the street to the Citizens Bank."

The office of the president of the Citizens Bank and Trust Company was in the center of the lobby of the bank. No private office, no partitioned space, no platform just a desk in the middle of things. Ted Holt was in his 70s, at least, and he had a number of notes, probably his "To Do" list, clipped under his tie clasp. "Hello, Peter. And you must be James Harrington, eh? Nice to meet you. What can I do for you boys?"

Lantinga told Mr. Holt the story from the beginning, including the "offer" made by the president of the bank across the street.

Mr. Holt listened intently, and Peter finished by asking if the bank would like to handle CORE's facility (all their banking business, including the loan).

Mr. Holt looked at them intently until he said, "Boys, I think we ought to pray about this." And with that, Mr. Holt folded his hands and bowed his head and in a sonorous voice that could heard throughout the lobby of the bank, began to pray—that's right—out loud.

"Our dear heavenly Father, we approach the throne of grace seeking Your wisdom and guidance in the matter before us. We beseech Thee, Heavenly Father," and the prayer continued, and continued, until the "Amen" no few minutes later.

Harry kept his hands folded and his eyes closed for the duration, but he could tell that whatever other business was being conducted in that bank's lobby had come to a silent standstill.

When he finished the prayer, Mr. Holt unfolded his hands, adjusted the notes under his tie clasp, and looked first at Harry and then at Peter and said, "I think the bank would like to help you boys out of this dilemma."

***

It was an incredulous and happy Harry that night who related the story to Lisa from beginning to end. When he was finished, Lisa exclaimed, "That's mind-boggling! He prayed right out loud?"

"You can't make this stuff up," Harry responded. "I know that loan officers have questionnaires in their desk drawers with a list from which they play twenty questions. The applicant will need to be able to answer most of the questions in the affirmative, or the loan will be denied. Questions like "Does the loan meet the bank's market focus?" and "What is the company's capacity to repay the funds?" and "What is the default risk of this loan?" and on and on. Instead, this loan officer prayed. Actually, this gives me some confidence the purchase of the equipment is the right thing to do, and I will be able to repay the loan. At least, God thinks so. He apparently told Mr. Holt to approve the loan."

CHAPTER TWELVE

Administrative Professionals, LLC. (Ad Pro) continued to grow. Kenneth Dekker left for a similar position with a much larger company in Colorado, and his replacement had been successful in attracting several new large clients. With that growth, there were now 155 associates and $1.5 million in pre-tax profit. Megan Sutter's addictions had grown as well. She had more grandchildren, spent more time in her home on Lake Michigan, and had been diagnosed with lung cancer. The surgery to remove the lower lobe of her left lung had been described by the doctors as successful. She appeared to be cancer-free, but she was warned that continued smoking could mean an untimely death.

She decided to put Ad Pro on the market so she could concentrate even more on her first two addictions. Because her officers were in no better position to buy her out than previously, she contacted David McTavish.

After reviewing her most recent financial statements, David advised her that the asking price should be $6 million and that he

JAY M. BYLSMA AND RANDY RUA

knew of no qualified buyers in Michigan, but he was aware there were several similar companies in the Chicago area that might have an interest. His network included an intermediary in Chicago who would be able to help.

She advised him she was in cancer recovery mode, which was the equivalent of "beach rest," and that he should work through John Davis, her Vice President of Finance. She gave John's contact information to David.

***

Benny Krautman was the intermediary David had in mind.

"Benny! Long time no see. David McTavish here. How are you and Sadie?"

"David McTavish? I should live so long to hear your voice again. We're well, thanks be to God. Thanks for asking. And how's by you?"

"The only way I could be better is if I were younger and better looking, and every day I grow farther from that goal!"

"Oy, I shouldn't have asked. What can I do for you, my friend?"

"I have a third-party human resources administrator for sale and looking for a buyer. It's about a $6-million deal, 150 employees, great client base, and it makes money."

"Mmmh. That's interesting! One of my poker buddies has Requirement, Inc. in Lincolnshire. Big firm, and I've helped him with another buyout. He might be ready for another. I'm ready to take some money from him to make up for my poker losses to him. I'll give him a call and get back to you."

"I look forward to hearing from you."

***

Requirement, Inc. was indeed a large player in the third-party human resources administrator marketplace. With over a thousand employees, it served several mega-clients in the Chicago area, including Sears and Boeing. So, Benny invited his friend to a pre-poker dinner, showed him a summary of Ad Pro's financial statements, and presented the $6-million asking price. Jonathan Rickman gambled on more than poker. It was a big reason for his success, and he saw Ad Pro as a sure thing. He advised Benny he was more than interested. Krautman promised to send over a Non-Disclosure Agreement the next day and, on receipt of a signed copy, would send over complete financials and other pertinent information.

"I want to see their client list, billing rates, and an organizational chart."

"I have that information and more. You can have it tomorrow. Now let's go play poker. I'm feeling lucky tonight!"

***

As promised, Megan Sutter concentrated on her recovery and left the negotiations up to John Davis.

The negotiation for the sale of a business is not for the faint-hearted. It begins with a verbal expression of interest, a signed Confidentiality Agreement, and the issuing of all manner of operational and financial information, including tax returns. Then, assuming the interest continues, a Letter of Intent to buy. The terms of the LOI are then accepted or refined (renegotiated), a sales document is prepared, and the buyer spends considerable energy performing "due diligence" to satisfy himself the information presented and on which the offer is based is true and accurate. Then a closing date is set.

In most cases, if the buyer has questions or concerns, he relates them to his intermediary, who communicates them to the seller's intermediary, and the questions or concerns get passed along to the seller. After the sales document are in progress, one can add an attorney to each end of the communication chain. If everyone in the chain had the goal of a successful conclusion, this can go smoothly. There has been an occasional case where, well, a closing didn't happen. All for good and proper reasons. Of course.

In this case, the few hiccups that normally surface did, and although it took working once through the night and once through the weekend, John was able to provide information to the buyer's and or his attorney's satisfaction, and three months from the pre-poker dinner meeting, a closing date was set—the Friday corresponding to the month's end upcoming in seven days. And everyone was allowed to take a well-deserved sigh of relief and did so—except John Davis.

***

It was late Wednesday morning when Megan Sutter placed her beach chair in such a way as to have the incoming waves soak her feet and yet not splash up onto the book she was reading, and her maid called to her from the front porch. "Ms. Sutter, there's a phone call for you, and the man said it was really important." She left her chair where it was and returned to the house.

"Ms. Sutter, David McTavish here. I'm afraid I have some bad news. John Davis has passed away. Apparently, it was a heart attack brought on by stress. I need you to come to my office as soon as it's convenient so we can make arrangements for the closing of the sale tomorrow. Could you possibly come this afternoon?"

When she arrived a McTavish's office, his conference room was spread with documents. The Confidentiality Agreement, the LOI, the attorney's engagement letter, the Sales Document, and the Closing Statement. And the company's attorney was present.

Her mind was racing. *What am I supposed to do? I left everything up to Davis, and he was supposed to meet with me on Thursday—tomorrow—to fill me in on everything. Now he's gone. I know nothing about this deal. I will be signing everything without knowing anything. I'm not ready. This is all so sudden. Poor John. Did the stress of this really cause his heart attack? Good God, I made him do this. Did I kill him? I can't even think straight. This is too much to process right now. I need a cigarette.*

Without the advice and consent of her trusted VP of Finance, John Davis, Megan Sutter refused to sign the Agreement to Purchase, and the deal was off.

As was David McTavish's $160,000 fee.

CHAPTER THIRTEEN

"This is an example of one of the five "D" reason for selling a business: Dispute." –Randy Rua

Lester LaGrande left the comfortable log cabin on his small private lake every morning at 5:30 to drive his Jeep Cherokee the 15 minutes to the shop he and his brother owned. He called it a shop, but with 80,000 square feet and 500-ton presses, it was, as his brother liked to call it, a manufacturing facility. He and his brother had inherited the shop equally from their father some ten years ago upon his death. Their mother still worked there; she was the bookkeeper.

Lester was VP of Manufacturing; his brother James was President and handled sales and engineering. He was the one with the college degree, while Lester had gone to work with his father at the shop right out of high school. Lester and James could not be more different. Lester wore jeans and a denim shirt; James (never Jim) wore Armani suits and drove a Maserati. James lived in a gated community and had his house programmed so that the lights and the stereo came on when he drove in the driveway. Lester drank Coors; James savored Domaine Drouhin Pinot Noir at $60 a bottle, and his 49% share of the income from the manufacturing facility allowed for that and more.

Since their father's death, the business had grown substantially, largely through James's sales efforts and his insistence they purchase ever larger capacity stamping presses and automatic feeding equipment. James kept selling, and Lester kept the equipment humming. Through these efforts, they had become a major supplier to a local Tier Two automotive supplier.

This morning was like every other morning for Lester until he tried his key in the lock at the employee entrance. It didn't work. He walked around to the office entrance, and it didn't work there either. Walter Smith, his first shift foreman was driving into the employee parking lot when Lester got back to the employee entrance. Walter was showing up a bit early, Lester thought. And from the look on Walter's face when he got out of the car, Lester knew something was different. What he found out in a few minutes was that something was a lot different.

"Morning, Walter. I hope you brought your keys."

"Morning, Lester. I did."

"I hope they work better than mine."

"Lester, I'm sorry to be the one to tell you, but—" he cut himself short at the sight of a police cruiser driving into the parking lot.

Lester approached the officer as he got out of the cruiser. "Hello, officer. Can I help you?"

"Are you Lester LaGrande?"

"I am."

"I'm here to enforce a court order to escort you off the property."

"A what? That can't be. I'm a half owner in this property. You can't kick me off. And what's more, I'm not going."

"According this court order, I have to. I'm sorry, Mr. LaGrande, but you have two choices. You can leave of your own accord and stay away, or I'll be forced to arrest you, and you can sort it out in a jail cell. Your choice."

***

The manufacturing facility was humming smoothly when James LaGrande arrived at 9:00. Lester LaGrande was seething at the offices of John Carter, Attorney at Law.

"He can't do that to me. I own as much stock in the company as he does."

"He can, and he did. He is counting on your mother's 2% of the stock to be voted in his favor to fire you. And frankly, there is nothing we can do legally to prevent it. He went to the court and convinced a judge that you are incompetent and a danger to the business, got the injunction, and had the locks changed. That he can do. What he can't do is cut you out of your share of the profits.

"This court order was entered by an attorney I'm familiar with. I've called his office to see what the official story behind this is, but he is in court this morning and likely will not get back to me until after lunch. I suggest you go home and come back at three o'clock, and by that time some of the dust will have settled and perhaps we can determine a plan of action. But do not go back to the shop. Don't even drive by. Are we clear?"

***

The attorney who filed the court order on behalf of James was Ted Dougherty, a principal in a large regional law firm.

"Ted. John Carter here. May I ask what's behind this LaGrande thing?"

"Thanks for calling, John. Here's what I'm authorized to tell you. James feels Lester's contribution to the success of the business pales in comparison to his contribution and resents Lester being paid an executive salary rate comparable to his for foreman's work. He doesn't feel Lester is necessary to the operation and even is a detriment as he doesn't stay current with manufacturing trends. He also alleges Lester has been negligent in his duties, causing some down time. He also believes his mother will vote with him if need be."

"A whole new definition of 'brotherly love' and being your brother's keeper. What is his intention for Lester's stock? I can't imagine touchy-feely times at the next shareholder's meeting."

"Or Christmas parties. I'm not at liberty to discuss James's wishes for that. The options obviously are limited to buying Lester out, or not buying him out and letting him sit with his stock."

"Based on James's actions so far, I'm sure Lester will trust him to do what's best for James with little or no thought for Lester. Well, thanks for your time. I'm meeting with Lester this afternoon, and we'll decide a course of action. I'm sure you'll be hearing from us."

***

Lester arrived at 2:30 that afternoon and was no less agitated than he was that morning. "What can I do to that bastard? What are my options? I want my job back!"

"Lester, you have two options. One is to do nothing; simply retain your 49% interest in the business. The other option is to seek to have James buy you out at a fair price, and you go your way and put the company behind you and get on with your life."

"That's not good enough. That gives James his way. What about suing for wrongful discharge?"

"I believe that would not have a favorable outcome and only cost you money. Even though you are an owner, you are what the law calls 'an employee at will,' which means your employer can fire you for any or no reason, just like you can quit for any or no reason."

Lester sat back in his seat and began chewing a fingernail. "So, what's left for me to do?"

"If you have the most recent financial statements, I suggest we hire a business appraiser and find out what your share might be worth. That may give us some guidance as to a path to pursue."

"I do."

"Get them to me as soon as you can and, in the meantime, stay away from the shop."

"What about my tools? I'd like to get my tools."

"Are they yours? Did you pay for them and bring them into the shop?"

"No, but over the years I collected a nice set of hand tools, and I'd like to get them."

"I'll see what I can do about the hand tools."

"Thanks. That would mean a lot to me."

***

John Carter had worked with David McTavish on a client's acquisition and was impressed with his work. He might be able to help here.

"David McTavish? John Carter here. How are you getting along these days? Still have your hand in an acquisition or two?"

"Hello, John. Nice to hear from you. I could use an acquisition or two. I hope you're calling needing some help in that arena."

"Well, I need your help with an acquisition of sorts. I need a quick and dirty business appraisal."

"I can do a quick one, a dirty one usually takes a little longer and costs a lot more. What do you have?"

***

The quick appraisal was that the company was worth $7 million. The dirty part was that a reluctant seller could contend that all manner of discounts could and should apply. Up to a 30% discount could apply because the stock was not marketable (like the stock in a listed company that could be sold anytime on the open market) and that a 49% interest should be further discounted for the lack of control (a minority shareholder has no power to influence company policy—as Lester was finding out in facing James). So, it could be argued that 49% of $7 million, or $3.4 million, should only be worth $1.8 million, if that.

McTavish's advice to Carter was to propose $3.4 million and if the discounts were brought up, the answer was that the stock was marketable, James was the buyer, and there should be no discount for a lack of control but rather a premium because the purchase would give James, an existing minority shareholder, a controlling interest.

And argued it was, for four months until McTavish received another call from Carter.

"David, I need you to take another look at Lester's position. We just received a six-month income statement, and the revenue and income have dropped off significantly. We will need another appraisal.

"What caused this sudden downturn? The economy is strong."

"Lester thinks this lack of revenue is James purposefully making the company look bad so the price he has to pay comes down."

Another look verified the price coming down, whether by deliberate means or not. The new valuation was $4.5 million, and it came with James's latest offer to buy Lester's 49% interest for $1.2 million. When David broke the bad news in the meeting with Lester and John Carter, Lester went ballistic and the language that came forth was unprintable, assuming these words might be read aloud in mixed company. Translated: Lester was not going to go away for $1.2 million.

After a moment of silence finally ensued, David offer a suggestion.

"You believe it is James's endgame to have all the company to himself?"

"And all the income, yes."

"And his biggest customer is the Tier Two automotive supplier?"

"Yes. Where are you going with this?"

"I happen to know the president of that company. We go back a ways; in fact, he was a wrestling opponent in high school. I helped him purchase a small electronics firm so he could control their supply to him. He may very well be interested in having a significant ownership interest in this facility—a major supplier. If we offer Lester's stock to him, and he has the least bit of interest, it may make James a bit more willing to see the light as regards the value of Lester's interest and come to the table with a better offer. Lester, I would need your permission to talk to my acquaintance. And if I'm right, James may find out he is wrestling with the wrong opponents."

***

David got an appointment with the president of the major customer, whose only question was, "Why is it for sale now? I've approached James LaGrande several times in the past to see if the company might be for sale."

When Ted Dougherty informed James of the Tier Two president's offer to buy 49% for $1.2 million or all of it for $2.4 million, it was James's turn to go ballistic. "My low-life brother had no business involving my customer . . ."

James's new offer was $3 million.

For Lester, the fishing on his small lake is best around 5:30 in the morning, and you should see his bass boat. He tricked it out with his really nice set of hand tools.

CHAPTER FOURTEEN

Harley Adams was known as a very astute businessman who ran a widely known electrical supply business, which bore his name. His customers loved him for his fairness, his competition respected him for his honesty, and his pastor relied on him for his generosity. His wife knew him to be frugal; his employees thought of him as parsimonious. The joke in the lunchroom was that Adams could fertilize a garden with what he could squeeze out of a buffalo nickel. So, while he paid above the minimum wage, no employee thought he or she made a maximum wage.

Franklin Page was the head of Outside Sales, and in his role, he was responsible for the firm's largest accounts, which were mostly large commercial and industrial contractors. He was paid a small basic salary and a commission, which in a good year would amount to $55,000. His 50-hour-a-week efforts on behalf of the company accounted for somewhere north of $3.5 million, about 15% of the company total. He had calculated his salary was $11.00 per hour, less than a penny for each dollar in sales he generated. Or in simple terms, not enough, a burden he carried home with him, too often, according to Mrs. Page, who encouraged him to "get happy or get out."

So, when Page learned State Street Electrical Supply was for sale, he contacted their broker, David McTavish.

State Street was smaller than Adams, largely because it had not penetrated the large commercial and industrial contractors, and Page was confident that with his contacts in that world, this would be a great opportunity. He signed the Non-Disclosure Agreement for himself and Mrs. Page, and together they kept an appointment to tour the business and meet the owner.

Mr. and Mrs. O'Donald ran a very nice business. State Street's inventory area was immaculate, their records were impeccable, and while their net income was considerably smaller than Adams', it was considerably larger than what Page was currently making. The asking price of $900,000 gave Page a bit of pause, but there was at least $500,000 in inventory and $100,000 in Accounts Receivable, which would be bankable. Page was encouraged that this might be just what he was looking for, although on his meager salary, he had accumulated few resources to put toward the purchase.

But the clincher was Page noticed that Mr. O'Donald wore a pin that indicated he was member of the Knights of Columbus, a Catholic fraternal order that does charity work on behalf of the Roman Catholic Church. In fact, O'Donald was a member of the Fourth Degree Assembly, which entitled him to be addressed as "Sir Knight." The Pages were also practicing Catholics, and a very strong bond was immediately formed.

On leaving, Page informed McTavish of his interest and asked what his next steps would be and was informed he should determine an appropriate offer, secure indications of bank financing if needed, and have a Letter of Intent (LOI) drafted. If O'Donald accepted the terms of the LOI, Page would proceed to do his due diligence while a sales agreement was drafted and accepted by both parties, and then a closing.

"How long should that take?"

"It can be done in a month if everything goes without a hitch. But plan on two to three."

"Then I won't quit my day job just yet."

***

It didn't close in a month, or in two. It seemed the delays were interminable, but at least one side or the other thought each delay necessary. Plus, it took a while to get a second mortgage on his home for $100,000, what with inspections and appraisals. Several well-to-do relatives had to "think about it a while" before agreeing to loan Page a total of $200,000. It was the third bank he and McTavish approached that agreed to provide up to $500,000 based on current inventory and Accounts Receivable. It took weeks for the bank to decide if it would be a commercial loan or Small Business Loan. Page was also prepared to max out their credit cards. He could just make the deal if O'Donald would take $90,000 as a Covenant Not to Compete, payable monthly over a five-year period. The O'Donalds needed time to consult with their accountant about the tax consequences of that proposal.

A due-diligence physical inventory revealed almost $70,000 of parts in the inventory that hadn't moved in six months. The bank insisted on discounting what they called "slow moving or obsolete" inventory that the O'Donalds insisted were seasonal and purchased at a substantial discount below cost and would not consider a corresponding reduction of the asking price.

And so it went, week after painful week. This or that issue would come up and be discarded or the sale price would be adjusted until on August 4, Cynthia Page awoke in the middle of the night in a cold sweat. St. Bartholomew had visited her in a dream and told her that unless something important in her life was not finished by his birthday, she should burn all her papers in a hot fire. It was clear to her that meant if the deal was not closed by August 24 (the Saint's birthday), they should call the purchase of State Street Electric off. To her, St. Bartholomew had given the deal a sign. It should close in twenty days or they were to back away as it didn't have the blessing of God and the Saints of the Church, and being a good Catholic woman, the dream was as good as an in-the-flesh meeting.

Page told McTavish of the deadline, who promised to work tirelessly to accomplish the closing. August being the month of vacations for lawyers, accountants, legal assistants, and bank loan officers, August 24 came and went without the closing, despite McTavish's best efforts. The Pages backed away, and the deal fell through, although Cynthia didn't insist all the paperwork be incinerated. Franklin Page continued working at Adams Electric.

David McTavish just shook his head. All that hard work, and he lost a $90,000 commission due to a religious woman's dream and a saint's birthday; a saint, he later learned, who was the Saint of Florentine cheese merchants.

He would have understood Cynthia Page's "dream" better if he had known that when the deal appeared to be closing soon, Franklin Page felt he had an obligation to give Harley Adams two weeks' notice so he could walk into State Street as its owner on the closing day. As mentioned before, Adams was an astute businessman. On reflection of Page's announcement, he reckoned he had a few buffalo nickels to spare as he didn't have a garden. He offered Page a raise that had the potential of tripling his take-home pay.

Mrs. Page dreamed happily ever after.

CHAPTER FIFTEEN

"Do you cut your own hair? Do you pull your own teeth? Why would you trust something as important as selling your life's work in a million-dollar transaction to an inexperienced, uninformed neophyte? Yes, you are the neophyte!" –Jay M. Bylsma

David Singleton was the youngest of four brothers growing up on a farm in rural Michigan. And the farm was in his blood. He loved the smell of newly overturned sod and freshly cut hay. He reveled in the sights and sounds of the animals and the birth of a calf or a chick breaking out of an egg. But most of all he was fascinated by the machinery and the different metals that were cast, machined, bent, and drilled and fashioned together to make moving parts: cast iron, stainless steel, bronze, copper, and tin. And when it was clear that his older brothers were going to stay with the farm and there would be no room for him, upon graduation from high school, he enrolled in Michigan Tech to study metallurgy. He graduated in four years *magna cum laude*.

His first job was as a control engineer at a heat-treating facility in Western Michigan. Heat treating is the process of heating metal parts to over 1,800 degrees Fahrenheit and then quenching the heated part in a cooling bath of oil or liquid salt to alter the physical properties of the metal, such as make it malleable or change its hardness. The company he worked for only did oil quenching, and Singleton knew there was a need for liquid salt quenching in the area. He did some research and put together a proposal to purchase the equipment to expand into salt quenching. He approached the owner with his proposal, and while the owner was impressed with the proposal, he didn't want to spend the money.

At a heat-treating conference, Singleton ran into one of his college roommates who also studied metallurgy. Eduardo (Eddie) De Luca's father owned several heat-treating facilities in Northern Indiana. Eddie joined the business after graduation, and as fate would have it, his father died from a heart attack within a year leaving the business to Eddie.

Over a beer (or two), Singleton lamented how his vision for a salt quench facility had been shot down by his employer. De Luca asked him to send the proposal he had prepared and indicated an interest in funding such an operation—perhaps a joint venture or a partnership? Singleton sent De Luca the proposal but wrote it off as a pipe dream.

De Luca didn't think it was a pipe dream. He proposed he fund the startup and Singleton run it in a 50/50 partnership. Singleton hesitated. De Luca was a short man with what Singleton's father called a "short man's complex" that is, "make up in bluff and puff what you lack in stuff." And he was always "right" and had an AQ** in the 140s. Singleton remembered De Luca had the chutzpah to argue with his professors. But Singleton graduated with honors, and De Luca was rumored to have made it through with a C- average, plus a bit of his

** AQ = "Asshole Quotient"—not to be mistaken for "IQ."

father's money donated to the university's endowment fund. De Luca needed Singleton's knowledge and presence, and Singleton needed De Luca's money. It turned out to be a match . . . made in Hell.

Singleton rented a building, bought their first piece of salt quench equipment, and started looking for work. He knew a local manufacturer of garment hangers sent their spring clips all the way to Detroit for salt-quench heat treating. They were his first customer.

Fast forward 15 years, and the business had grown to a sizable salt quench facility and had an oil quench facility in a smaller town some 60 miles away.

***

At church one Sunday, a fellow vestry member approached David McTavish. "I work for the partner of a heat-treating facility who is suffering from what I call 'industrial depression.' His partner beats up on him mercilessly for no apparent reason. He needs someone to talk to, and I recommend he call you."

McTavish was surprised, "Me? I'm not an industrial psychologist."

"I know. But I think you could help him. If he calls, talk to him as a favor to me. It could make my life at this job a lot less stressful. His name is David Singleton."

Several days later, Singleton did call. McTavish went to see him.

His office was interesting. He had a large saltwater fish tank (to help him calm his nerves in stressful times) and an airplane propeller mounted on a large board. One arm of the propeller was bent at a 90° angle.

McTavish broke the ice. "I'll bet there's a story behind that bent propeller?"

"There is. I'm a pilot, actually, and the company owns a Piper.

One time on an approach, I forgot to set the landing gear down, and that propeller was the first thing to hit the ground. Every time I see that plaque, I remind myself to remember what's important in life."

"Apparently it wasn't a fatal mistake."

"No. There is a saying, 'There are old pilots and there are bold pilots, but there are no old bold pilots.' I want to be an old pilot."

And they got down to business. McTavish spent two hours listening. According to Singleton, besides De Luca berating him in front of the employees for running a lousy operation (that incidentally made a lot of money), De Luca was using the partnership as a way to cheat on his wife. He bought vacation property and put it into the partnership to hide the purchase. Then he told his wife he needed to come to Michigan on weekends to oversee Singleton's "problem operation," only to spend the time with his paramour. When Singleton would see Gwen, Eddie's wife, at heat treating conferences, he couldn't look her in the eye.

McTavish suggested some approaches that might make life easier between Singleton and his partner, and sent him a bill for $200. The bill was paid promptly.

Several months later, Singleton called again. The first meeting was very helpful and caused Singleton to see things differently; would McTavish be willing to come again?

This time McTavish broached the subject of Singleton buying out De Luca.

"He'd never sell."

"Everything is for sale. We just need to know the terms and the price."

Singleton leaned back in his chair and let out a big sigh. "It would take a huge load off my back. How would we go about doing it? I don't have very much money laying around, and he won't sell cheap."

"The business is asset rich and has a wonderful cash flow. That means the possibility of considerable bank financing. I wouldn't doubt you could finance a portion of a buyout by selling off the oil quench facility."

Singleton was incredulous. "You really think so? What would we need to do?"

"First, allow me to do a quick and dirty appraisal as to what the two facilities are worth and an estimate as to how far a bank might be willing to finance you. Then we'll devise a plan to approach De Luca."

***

The appraisals estimated the oil quench facility to be worth $1.2 million and the salt quench facility to be over $5 million. McTavish thought Singleton's bank could be persuaded to go as high as $4 million, collateralizing the equipment, accounts receivable, and real estate.

"Where am I going to come up with the $2.2-million shortfall?"

"You are going to ask De Luca to carry paper."

"He'll never do it."

"We don't know until we ask. And here's how you're going to ask. Fly down to Indiana and tell De Luca you want to buy him out. Mention that you are both getting older, and you are certain De Luca doesn't want to have to deal with your wife if you were to die, nor does he want to have to explain the vacation property to his wife. You think it's time to settle affairs—no pun intended. Tell him you don't have the cash, but with bank financing and your long-standing friendship, you are certain De Luca would be willing to hold some paper. Do not come close to mentioning what we think the businesses are worth."

"He'll never do it."

***

The meeting was ugly. After Singleton made his pitch, De Luca just stared at him for what seemed like an eternity. Then he blew his top. "After all I've done for you, David. Carried your sorry ass through good times and bad, not to mention financing you at the beginning. You f***king ungrateful, sorry son of a bitch. I'll let you buy me out, but it will be cash. I won't carry a nickel of your paper. It will be $2 million and not a penny less. Now get out of my sight."

Singleton called McTavish from a phone booth when he go back to the airport.

"I told you he wouldn't do it. And I've really pissed him off. I don't want to think about his next visit to the shop. Besides, I don't think you are correct in your appraisal. Eddie is a smart man in this business; he thinks his half of the business is only worth $2 million."

"Come home and we'll talk further, and remember you want to be an old pilot."

***

"Here's an easy way to see whose opinion of value is correct," McTavish said when they met. "Go to your bank, explain what you want to do, and see how far they are willing to go to back you."

After meeting with the bank, Singleton reported in. "The bank will go as far as $3.5 million on both facilities. I cheerfully apologize for questioning your judgment. So, what do we do now?"

"I go see De Luca and see if I can persuade him to lower the price and accept your paper."

"He'll never do it."

"Seems I've heard that from you before. My purpose in seeing him is not to change his mind. I hope to cement the $2-million price in his mind."

After the meeting with De Luca, it occurred to McTavish if he were smaller and De Luca were bigger, De Luca would have physically thrown McTavish out of his office. ". . . and the f***king $2 million is in cash, or no motherf***king deal," was one of the nicest things De Luca said.

***

The deal was consummated at $2 million in cash, and De Luca got the vacation property and put it into a dummy corporation. The oil quench facility sold within six months for $1.2 million, and the salt quench facility sold a year later for $5.8 million. After paying off the $2-million bank loan he took out to pay De Luca, Singleton netted $5 million. He donated $1 million to Michigan Tech, put $1 million each into two charitable remainder trust for himself and his wife, and with some of the rest he bought a working farm.

Oh, the smell of new-mown hay.

But the highest moment of elation came at the next heat-treating conference when he bumped into Eduardo De Luca. "Singleton," he said, "damn you. You're going to buy me a drink, maybe two. And we're going to reminisce fondly about how you badly you screwed me over with our deal. I found out the hard way that you *cum laudes* are a lot smarter than I ever thought you were."

Oh, the sweet taste of *schadenfreude*.

CHAPTER SIXTEEN

"Of the '5 Ds' reasons for selling a business:
Distress, Dispute, Disability, Divorce, and Death,
try to avoid the last one." –Randy Rua

The increase in government regulations in the field of Human Resources (a new reg. came out almost daily) helped Administration Professionals, LLC. (Ad Pro) to continue to grow. In addition, Megan Sutter decided to add a department to write proprietary computer code so the firm could extend their services to include administering payroll. Internet connectivity and networking further provided platforms for growth. Revenue had risen to nearly $10 million, and net income for the past fiscal year was only a little short of $2 million, generated by 250 employees.

For Megan Sutter, business was good, but her health wasn't. After being cancer free for two years, a six-month check-up showed the cancer had begun to metastasize into her bones. There had been no major physical signs at first, but ever so slowly, she began noticing an unexplained ache here or there until the check-up confirmed the reason for the aches and pains. She followed a protocol for radiation and then chemotherapy. Her experience was the treatment was often worse than the cancer as it made her very weak and nauseous, and she lost her hair. But she was resolved to fight this battle to the last, even if it was to be the last.

After the treatments, a CAT scan showed some remission of the cancer, but it was not complete, and it had spread to her adrenal glands. She wasn't given much time, six months at the outside.

She called David McTavish. This time it was a southern Ohio company that had an interest, and this time Sutter took control of the negotiations and was in the thick of it, stressful though it was.

Four months and $30,000 worth of legal bills later, the closing date arrived. In a large conference room at the local title company sat her team: two lawyers from her law firm, her in-house lawyer, her VP of Finance, and David McTavish. She was too tired to count how many were there from the buyer's side, but she nodded in appreciation at Richard Troutman, their very nice president—he had been a real gentleman.

Papers were passed around to be signed, and after the pens were put down, Troutman concluded the ceremony with a short tribute to Megan Sutter's accomplishments in growing Ad Pro to one of the outstanding operators in the field of third-party human resource management, and there was a round of applause. He continued to assure Sutter they would work assiduously to live up to the standards she had set in service to her customers. With that and good wishes, Troutman and his entourage left the room.

When she spoke words of appreciation to her teammates, she couldn't control the emotions she felt, and the words were husky. When she turned to McTavish, she said, "David, thank you for putting up with this old biddy all these years. What has it been, nine or ten? And it took us three times to get it right? I have a word of

YOU JUST CAN'T MAKE THIS STUFF UP...

advice to pass along to your clients. Tell them it's much harder to get out than it is to get in. And now gentlemen, if you don't mind, I'd like to ask to be excused from the nice celebratory luncheon we have planned. This old biddy is tired and needs to get some rest."

When her will was read only three months later, besides some personal things and the Lake Michigan property, there was $8 million in cash to be distributed. $1 million went to a selection of her former employees, more to those who had been with her longer, and even more to key players who were instrumental in helping her grow the company. Another million was dispersed among several favorite charities. Another million went to her church's endowment fund, and $5 million was divided between the National Cancer Institute and the American Cancer Society, with the stipulation the money be spent for research into bone cancer. When any of these recipients thought of Megan Sutter, the phrase "Old Biddy" didn't come to mind.

She also left instructions that the following inscription be placed on her tombstone:

"For the want of a cigarette, a fortune was lost."

R.I.P. Megan Sutter

CHAPTER SEVENTEEN

SOMETIME IN 2005

"Of the '5 Ds' reasons for selling a business: Distress, Dispute, Disability, Divorce, and Death, one of them can be truly distressing . . . if it happens to you." –Randy Rua

"Never try to get the last nickel out of an investment." –Jay M. Bylsma (Sixth Rule for Successful Investing)

Wie probeert te krijgen met de laatste druppel uit de pot krijgt de deksel op zijn neus."***–Anna Bylsma (Jay's Dutch Grandmother)

Don Foster's forward-thinking idea that the construction industry needed to computerize Gantt and PERT charts was correct. Critical paths were best trod by dedicated on-site software programs supported by on-site servers, and his company, Construct Data, provided both for small to midsize construction companies. Founded in 1990, it had grown to $10.5 million in sales and generated

$3.2 million in cash flow. His growth was largely financed by pledging his receivables as he was only too happy to finance an ever more opulent lifestyle with the company's earnings.

He had heard of David McTavish from a golfing buddy, who had just sold his business through David, and decided to call him to find out if and when he could play golf full-time like his buddy.

The meeting with McTavish was just what he wanted to hear. The business would be worth in the neighborhood of $12 million, which was a neighborhood Foster could live in (with careful budgeting). But while 2005 was a blockbuster year, with the new business being bid on, 2006 would bust whatever records 2005 eventually set.

"This is my retirement, David. I don't have a 401k or IRA. This business is my retirement account. I estimate 2006 will be $12.5 million in sales and nearly $4 million in cash flow. What would the value be if I waited to sell until after 2006?"

McTavish estimated $15 million.

Foster made two decisions. One was to wait until after 2006 to put the business up for sale, and the other was to begin construction on a $1.8-million dream home on Lake Milner—actually on the seventh hole of a golf course that tracked around the south end of Lake Milner. He would be able to retire honing his skills on his two avocations, golf and fishing. Actually three avocations, the third was to watch new movie releases in the movie theater that would occupy the space under the four-stall garage.

The next time McTavish visited Don Foster was in the spring of 2007. And Don Foster was ready to sell. No, eager to sell—actually desperate to sell. He had not seen that the construction bubble he was riding was going to burst in 2006; he didn't react to it soon enough, and his optimism that the decline in construction was a small blip turned out to be wrong, fatally wrong. McTavish agreed to represent Foster in the sale of Construct Data. When the new price was determined, one shoe dropped. The newly estimated value was $3 million, based on $1.5 million in Accounts Receivable and $1.5 million in computer equipment, servers, and Construct Data's proprietary software. Worse, cash flow was barely enough to make payroll. At $3 million, he would be able to pay the taxes, finish the dream home, and set up a retirement account, meager as it was going to be.

The other shoe dropped when the bank told Foster they were calling in the loan that financed the $1.5 million in Accounts Receivable. When McTavish heard of the bank's action, he went to see the presiding loan officer.

"If I can effect a sale, the bank will come out whole," McTavish argued. "If you foreclose on the A/R, we might as well hold an auction, and a very nice business will evaporate."

"Do you have anything positive in the works?" asked the loan officer.

"I was called in only four days ago. The ink in the Memorandum of Offering is not dry yet. So, no."

The loan officer held firm. "This recession is hitting every construction company hard. Companies like the ones that own Foster money are declaring bankruptcy at a rate never before seen in my experience. The bank has to step in to protect itself. We will rely on Foster's personal guarantee to come out of this whole. I understand your stake in this. If there is no sale, there is no commission, and frankly, even if there was a commission on the Accounts Receivable, the bank wouldn't allow Foster to pay it. I'm truly sorry, but the Bank has no choice."

McTavish's reply was terse. "I understand your position and your reasoning. Please, understand mine. A careful reading of the sales agreement will show quite specifically that if the sale turns out to be an asset sale or a disposal of assets for value, there is a commission due on the sale of those assets to the extent of value received.

I frankly don't care who pays the commission, but I believe that sale document represents an enforceable contract you will have to honor, and you will not have clear title to those Accounts Receivable until and unless that contract is honored. Have a good day."

The computers, servers, and software netted a mere $235,000, which was less than the losses the bank sustained in the collection of the foreclosed $1.5 million in Accounts Receivable. Don Foster had to secure a construction loan to finish the house and then secure a mortgage to make up the difference of the Accounts Receivable loan and the amounts the bank was able to collect and honor his personal guarantee.

The economic downturn and the resulting drop in construction was depressing. The resulting plummet of the value of Construct Data was distressing. From a business worth $12 million to $1.2 million equity and a $600,000 mortgage on a $1.8-million mansion is hard to stomach just reading about it. Anna Bylsma was right.

***"He who tries to get the last drop out of the kettle will get the cover on his nose." Anna Bylsma*

CHAPTER EIGHTEEN

Maynard LaRue started his pigment and dye business in 1947 at age 25 with $500 he borrowed from his father. He was part of the occupation forces in West Germany after WWII and had fallen in love with a German girl whose father owned a pigment and dye business that was partially destroyed in the bombing of Frankfurt. Corporal LaRue had spent over a year and a half helping his future father-in-law rebuild the business in his spare time and learned some of his secrets, which he brought back to start his own business when his tour of duty was over.

LaRue's knowledge of the pigments and techniques for coloring the various plastic materials that were coming into play in both the automotive and appliance industries fueled steady growth for PP&D, Inc. (a/k/a Paramount Pigment & Dye, Inc.). Trips back to Germany for his wife to see her family allowed LaRue to trade technology and discoveries with his father-in-law. This kept both firms in the forefront of their industry in their respective countries.

Maynard and Greta had two sons. Fredrich, the oldest, was born color-blind (to the dismay of his father) and became a lawyer. Hans, the younger, was hanging around the company's chemistry laboratory before he was in high school. He got his degree in chemistry at Stanford in 1967 and returned to hang around in the company's laboratory full time.

Hans made several discoveries in chemical bonding that allowed for stronger bonds between the pigment or dye and the source material. That boosted PP&D's reputation, as well as their sales, nationally. Despite his company's reputation and growth, Maynard LaRue never forgot his roots and knew his success was dependent on a strong work force, in the lab and in each department. He knew all his employees and called them by name (names etched in everyone's uniform or lab smock helped him remember). He promoted from within, maintained the best benefit package money could buy, and matched his employees' 401k contributions by 50%. To his face, he was Mr. LaRue. Behind his back, he was affectionately known as Papa LaRue. It was appropriate; he considered them all his family.

Hans's only son, Edward, joined PP&D in 1988 upon his graduation from Wharton Business School. The proud father and grandfather posed for a photo with him to highlight an article in the industry's trade journal, *Pigment and Resin Technology*, entitled "A Legacy in Color." Edward majored in Accounting and Finance, and with $22 million in sales and 275 employees, there was plenty of accounting and finance to oversee.

Maynard, then aged 67, found plenty to keep himself busy. He still maintained a bench in the lab, and he called on key customers with whom he had maintained relationships with from the early days of the company—customers like General Electric and General Motors (he liked to say he was a corporal calling on the generals). He oversaw the planning of a new 540,000-square-foot facility and was in the general contractor's field office nearly every business day until it was completed. He didn't smoke or drink (much), and he could beat any of his progeny in racquetball and wasn't afraid to mention it.

The company maintained a steady annual growth rate of 5% to 6% annually and profitability rose proportionally. Their success and reputation attracted various suitors as well as venture capitalists, but after listening to their pitches, Maynard would decline their offers. None of the suitors appeared to be willing to commit to leaving the company as it was and where it was. In each case, PP&D would be absorbed, moved, and or dismantled. Papa LaRue would have none of it.

Edward LaRue's only son, Lawrence, worked summers at PP&D throughout college. And while he majored in Business Administration, he minored in Theater. During the summer of his junior year, his grandfather Hans retired and moved to Arizona. Just after Christmas the following year, his father prematurely died of a heart attack. When Larry arrived at PP&D after graduation in 2009, sales had risen to $61 million, and pretax profits were $7 million. He dove into the management team with the sense of responsibility that had been bred into him and a lack of enthusiasm he couldn't squelch. But he gave it his best shot for a year until the local theater company advertised for a Business Manager.

At age 88, Maynard was still the Chairman of the Board, the majority shareholder, and still puttered around at his bench in the lab. He joked that the dye business was in and had colored his blood. He met to mentor young Larry once a week as time permitted and was disappointed when Larry told him he was considering taking the theater's business manager's job. "I respect and cherish the opportunity to continue your legacy," he told his great-grandfather. "But I don't have the skill set to manage a $60-million company. And with my grandfather and father gone, I'm overwhelmed. And my heart's not in it. I'm so sorry to disappoint, but I would be doing you and the company a disservice by staying and pretending I was up to the task."

After the meeting, Maynard called David McTavish.

A week after the initial consultation, McTavish returned to meet with Maynard and his great-grandson. "The company has a value of between $24 million and $26 million, including the real estate, which I ballpark at $2.5 million. I'm a business valuator, not a real estate appraiser. We could hire an appraiser, but for right now, $2.5 million is close enough for the girls I date."

He was engaged to find a buyer, with instructions that a buyer who would preserve the LaRue legacy would be given preference over price. When McTavish pressed Maynard as to what that meant, tears came to Maynard's eyes and his voice broke. "There are employees that have been with me for forty years or more. We have over 750 employees, some of them several generations of families who rely on me for their livelihood. This company has a significant economic impact on this community. I don't want that to be disrupted or destroyed by having the place moved. Heavens knows it's not about the money. What is an eighty-eight-year-old going to do with a few extra million? And the family is already set financially. So, David, go find me a *good* buyer."

McTavish found several buyers. Buyer Number One was a venture capital firm whose offer was for 51% of the stock (Maynard's holding) for $15 million. PP&D would fit nicely into their platform of secondary suppliers to the Tier One automotive suppliers. They didn't have the cash to buy out all the stock but pledged the minority shareholders could and would be liquidated over a five-year period.

Maynard LaRue declined. "These people typically buy and sell businesses like some people flip houses. They drain the cash (over which the minority shareholders have no control) and bundle it with one or two other companies and sell it for higher multiples of earnings. That's how the minority shareholders get liquidated. No, thank you."

Buyer Number Two offered $22 million including the real estate. They indicated they were cautious buyers and cited the economic downturn of 2007 as the reason for the admittedly low bid. However, it was a family-owned business, and it came with a pledge to keep the company as it was, including its name.

Maynard LaRue was pleased they wanted the real estate—a good indication they would leave the company where it was and grow it from there with the existing employees. And they understood family-owned business. The legacy would be intact.

Buyer Number Thre offered $26 million and an agreement to lease the real estate.

Maynard LaRue knew leasing the real estate was a clear sign they were not willing to make a long-term commitment to keeping the company and its employees where they were. "Lawrence, 26 million for the stock and we keep the building. That amounts to $28.5 million versus buyer number two's offer of 22 million including the real estate. We'd be leaving $6.5 million on the table if we went with number two. What do you think?"

Larry had done his homework—for himself and for his mother. "Grandfather, the incremental millions don't mean much to you. At 51%, the difference is $3 million on top of $11 million. To me and my 16%, the incremental difference is significant. It's 1 million more than 3.5. That's enough to buy me a Paddle Pop or two."

Maynard thought for a moment. "I agree. $6.5 million is too much to leave on the table. So, we could say the company is worth $22 million, and the legacy is worth $6.5 million. Mmmm. Not a bad return on $500 investment. Did I ever tell you that my father died before I thought to pay the $500 back?"

CHAPTER NINETEEN

"If you fail to plan, you are planning to fail." –**Randy Rua**

When Henk DeVries immigrated to the US from the Netherlands in 1975, he was taken aback by the US system of weights and measures. Raised on the metric system, inches and feet were a mystery (a yard is the distance between King Henry I's nose and the tip of his thumb?). And when it came time to buy a set of tools to change the muffler on his VW, the only tools he could find were US/imperial, which were useless on the nuts and bolts on his VW. He had to import a set of spanners (wrenches) from Europe. And an idea for a business was born.

Initially, he kept his day job working in the shipping department of a local metal office furniture manufacturer. Nights and weekends, he called on auto body and auto repair shops as well as car dealerships that specialized in cars made in Europe. He would take orders for any tools that were required to be in metric, purchase the tools in Europe by long-distance telephone and deliver them when they arrived in this country.

As the business grew, he began stocking an inventory of the tools that were in highest demand and he quit his day job. It was largely his infectious enthusiasm and charisma that made his sales pitches hard to turn down.

***

Fast forward to 1999 and DeVries (now Metrek Tools, Inc.) had contracted with the Chinese firm Hebei Sinotools, Ltd. to forge and produce a complete line of hand tools in both metric and imperial and stamped with the Metrek logo. It was the largest distributor of metric hand tools in the Midwest, and one would be hard-pressed to enter a hardware store in the region and not find Metrek tools. And at age 60, it was Henk (now Hank) DeVries's enthusiasm and charisma that continued to fuel the company's growth. His employees joked he could charm the chrome off a screwdriver blade.

And at age 60 Hank was contemplating retiring and, wishing to seek out the best way to do it, he consulted David McTavish.

"Now is a good time to begin planning for a smooth exit. You want to be in control of when and how you exit. You want to be ready to exit if and when an opportunity presents itself. You will want to maximize what you put in your pocket. You will want to avoid unnecessary expenses and taxes—especially taxes. You will want to tell your family and your key employees that you are planning to exit.

"If you carefully plan to exit, you will beat the 95% failure rate of those who fail to plan, and the exit process will be far less stressful during the selling process."

"How long does this plan take?"

"As little as a year, or as long as it takes—maybe five years."

"How do I maximize what I put in my pocket?"

"What we will strive to do is focus on de-risking the business so that a buyer will pay the maximum price for the business, given its sales and profits."

After the meeting, DeVries had a plan divided into a checklist. He set about, as McTavish put it, "de-risking" the business.

The first item on the checklist was to find a second and perhaps third source of supply. As McTavish has put it, "Having only one source of supply for your tools puts you in a very high-risk situation. Particularly one in a communist country. Any prospective buyer would want to see several sources of supply."

DeVries went to the next hand tool exhibition in Shanghai and found Xuzhou Perfect Industry Technology, Inc., an ISO 9001 certified manufacturer. He also found a second source, T.J. & Grace, which looked to be a quality hand tool manufacturer located in Taiwan—which is not communist China. DeVries placed trial orders with both firms and was pleased with the results. Put a check by that item.

Also, T.J. & Grace had recently introduced a very appealing line of lithium battery-powered hand tools—power drills, power screwdrivers, power drivers, and various handheld saws. For sizeable orders, Grace would apply the Metrek brand. With the addition of this line of power tools, Metrek's sales spiked 15% the first year it was offered. Add a line, "Increase sales by expanding product offerings," to the list and put a check mark next to it.

One of the items on the checklist was to inform your family and employees of your plan to exit. His wife Laurie was a bit of a wanderlust. When Hank told her of the plan, she had only one question: "Will you get enough for the business so we can buy a motor home and can cruise the USA? I've always wanted to see the redwoods and get giddy on good wine in Napa Valley." His employees were less enthusiastic, but as one of them put it, "None of us really expected you to die in the saddle." Put a check by that item.

And so it went. Item by item, Hank focused his energy on continuing to grow the business, servicing his customers, and doing right by his employees, but now with an eye to the end game—the exit.

***

It was a bit more than three years after his first meeting with DeVries when McTavish phoned.

"Hank! David McTavish. How are you doing?"

After explaining that most of the items of the plan's checklist had a check or half a check mark, McTavish said, "That's good, because I have a buyer if you're ready to sell."

Actually, it turned out to be three buyers, and Hank told Laurie the good news. After listening, she had something thoughtful to say, "You shouldn't pick the buyer. You are a great salesman as evidenced by the company's success. But to you, everyone's a good customer, even a great customer. And not everyone is a good customer. And this isn't wrenches we're selling, when it doesn't matter if the customer is good or not. This is a multi-million-dollar business. You should rely on your intermediary to choose the best buyer, or even let me choose."

"You?"

"Yes, me. I'm a great judge of character. I chose you, didn't I?"

"You're joking, right?"

"Dead serious."

"Not that I'm agreeing to this, but how would you go about choosing the best candidate?"

"Let me think about that. But don't cut me out of this decision. I think you need me, Mr. 'I trust everybody.'"

***

Of the three potential buyers, two were cash buyers whose offers were within 2% of each other. The third offered 5% more but wanted DeVries to hold about 30% of the purchase price in a seven-year note, and so was ruled out. Buyer Number One was a good-looking, middle-aged man, a great dresser with a sparkling personality, and very verbal. He had just the kind of personality that could and should run a sales organization. The buyer behind door number two was a certified public account by background, and his personality fit what came to Hank's mind when he heard the profession called "bean counters." However, he was knowledgeable in the industry, having had a competitor of Metrek as a client. But a salesman he wasn't. When McTavish asked Hank how he would choose, he said, "I'm not. My wife is."

McTavish was incredulous, "Your wife? What does she—how did that come to be? How does she fit into the picture?"

"She is a good judge of character and is quick to point out that I'm not—not as good. Because the deals are the same economically, it will rest on who is the best-suited buyer, and I've agreed, albeit reluctantly, to allow her a say in the choice. She wants to invite each candidate and their wives to dinner, and she will decide based on those meetings."

"You're serious?"

"I'm not only serious, I'm in a delicate situation. This is sort of an Occam's razor. Besides, if I pick the wrong one, the silence will echo through the halls of my marriage to my dying day. If she picks the wrong one, there will be a shrug of the shoulders and a tacit admission neither of us was qualified to choose. Case closed."

David McTavish only shook his head. *You just can't make this stuff up*, he thought. "Good luck with that," he said.

***

Hank thought the dinner with Buyer Number One went very well. They were a good-looking couple and were at ease with themselves. He was charming, very well-spoken, and clearly ambitious. The man was the VP of a regional food broker. Hank thought the man could sell ice to Eskimos.

The dinner with Buyer Number Two was . . . nice. Whereas Buyer Number One wore a navy blazer and light blue button-down shirt without a tie, Buyer Number Two wore a grey suit and white shirt with a black and white striped tie. The wife was more loquacious then he, but he had a certain bonhomie and exuded confidence and strength. They were both on the intelligent side of being bright. The man was a CPA in a Big-Eight firm. Hank thought the man would see that Eskimos didn't need ice.

Laurie chose the CPA, to both Hank's and McTavish's dismay as Buyer Number One was their clear choice.

***

As it turned out, Buyer Number Two, Stephen Wright, foresaw the economic downturn of 2007. Something about Baby Boomers buying their last home at age 47, and the last of the Baby Boomers reaching at 47 in 2006 causing the housing bubble to burst and the ensuing downturn. He budgeted for it, made strategic plans for it, rode it out, and came out on the other side with a stronger company.

Buyer Number One was made the managing partner of the food brokerage business. He aggressively took on additional lines to represent, decided to inventory several hard-to-get items with long lead times, got over-extended, and when the downturn came, the business tanked.

When pressed as to what insight she had in choosing the CPA, she said it was easy. "I liked Lucy Wright's judgment better."

"And how did you know Mrs. Wright's judgment was better."

"She made the far better choice of husbands."

You just can't make this stuff up.

(Authors' note: We are aware some readers might think there is just a pejorative hint of sexism in the resolution of this chapter. Please know we don't make this stuff up, and we leave it to the reader to pass judgment on any inferences that can be drawn.)

CHAPTER TWENTY

The Seacord sisters inherited Allfast, Inc. from their father, who started the business when they were in middle school. Allfast was a fastener distributor in which they had helped almost from its beginning. After each received an Associate Degree in Business from the local community college, they joined their then-widowed father as full-time employees, Clarise (the gregarious sister) in Sales and Marjorie (the introvert) in Operations. Over time, and as their father aged, they assumed the roles, if not the titles, of Managing Partners. Because the times they saw eye-to-eye on any issue were rare, their father's major role was the arbitrator. And because he was the owner, and because he was fair, they abided by his decisions and all went smoothly—until he died and left the business to the sisters, 50% to each.

With the absence of their father, not only did discord grow, they also fought like alley cats. Important issues went undecided as their arbitrator had died and, to Marjorie's mind, their in-fighting was hurting the growth and development of the business. Their employees called it the Seacord Discord.

Jack Wentworth was the company's long-time CPA. In desperation, Marjorie sought his advice on an issue that had potential tax consequences. Clarise rejected his advice, believing he favored Marjorie's position and was not neutral.

Clarise went to the same church as David McTavish and sought his advice on yet another issue. It was not hard to guess the outcome of that advice; it was rejected by Marjorie as being biased toward Clarise. And so it went; as each large issue resulted in an impasse, it became harder to find an issue that was not worth a fight, right down to whether the purchase should be #2 or #2½ pencils.

And the business languished for the want of a decision-maker, an arbitrator, and pencils.

Finally, McTavish's advice to Clarise was either sell the business to a third party or buy out her sister to have a free hand to run the business as she wished. In order to remove any perceived bias, Clarise approached their CPA, Jack Wentworth, to advise her about what the value of the business might be. Wentworth acknowledged his practice didn't do business valuations, but as a ballpark number, he thought, based on the value of the Accounts Receivable and the fastener inventory, the value should be about $1 million.

Prepared with Wentworth's information, Clarise approached Marjorie with the offer either to put the business up for sale or to buy Marjorie's 50% interest for $500,000. As could be predicted, the mother of all catfights ensued. Clarise was accused of going behind Marjorie's back in dealing with Wentworth, and was she now willing to steal her share of the business for a mere $500,000? Did she have no respect for their father's legacy? Or to put it in three small words, "How could she?" or, in three other small words, "Go to hell."

Clarise's defense that she had used Wentworth only because Marjorie seemed to value his opinion and that it was his professional opinion, not hers, and all other arguments were to of no avail. And their personal rift deepened. They were now fighting like Bengal tigers.

Clarise went again to David McTavish, who declined to do a valuation. "What good would it do? Your sister will not accept anything you bring to the table."

"So, what's to be done?"

"Let me bring a buyer or two to the table and let them make an offer. Perhaps an offer from a third party will take away any bias that can be associated with you."

Business valuations are not like the market prices set by realtors for real estate where a buyer might pay more for the same house with an up-to-the-minute kitchen or an elaborate master bedroom suite or a view of Lake Michigan. Businesses are valued by the net present value of future earnings, which is typically calculated by applying a multiplier on the most recent established cash flow. So, it was no surprise when McTavish received two offers, both for within $50,000 of $1.1 million.

When Marjorie was presented with the offers, she agreed they should take $1.1 for the business, and she accepted Clarise's offer for $550,000.

Marjorie retired to tend to her one-acre dahlia garden. Clarise hired an Operations Manager and went on to grow the business and, in eight years, sold out to the Operations Manager for $3 million in cash and notes with the assets of the business as collateral.

It took three years after the Clarise bought out Marjorie before they and their families began to get together for Christmases.

After Clarise sold out, she was astute enough never to disclose the sale price to her beloved sister.

CHAPTER TWENTY-ONE

"If you choose not to use a professional intermediary to sell your business, it is rare someone will pay too much for your business; it is more likely you will not get enough." –Jay M. Bylsma

The electric-shock-like feeling when he moved his neck and the extreme fatigue that began to creep up on him around eleven o'clock in the morning was enough for John Overmier to call his primary care doctor for an appointment. He was referred to a neurologist, who put Overmier through a serious of tests to confirm his primary care doctor's preliminary diagnosis of relapsing-remitting multiple sclerosis, or MS.

"MS is a progressive disease," the neurologist warned. "But we have number of medications that can retard the progression significantly. While your life will never again be normal as you knew it, with proper medication, a bit of physical therapy, and as little stress in your life as possible, you can expect to live a long and fulfilling life. What do you do for a living?"

"I own a mid-sized plastic injecting molding company," Overmier answered.

***

OM Plastics, Inc. did $7 million in sales to a variety of customers in the automotive, medical, packaging, and hand tool industries. Typically, there were 95 employees operating 17 presses or molding cells on three shifts. Many of his presses were fitted with robotic unloaders that he had designed and were made in his extensive tool room. "As little stress as possible" was not possible for the owner and operator of OM Plastics, Inc.

Overmier had little choice but to hire a general manager to handle the day-to-day operations of the business. After an extensive search, the new president of OM Plastics was Robert Bainbridge. He had an engineering degree from the University of Michigan and an MBA from the University of Chicago. He was previously the VP of Engineering in a large plastic injection molding company and VP of sales in another. He was the perfect candidate, and although his asking salary of $150,000 was higher than Overmier wished to pay, he agreed to it.

The business didn't flourish under Bainbridge's management, but he worked hard enough to steer the company to 5% annual growth and from $150,000 to $200,000 in pretax profit. And this allowed John Overmier to live his life with "as little stress as possible." His MS did progress, but so slowly it was not readily discernable. His medication almost precluded relapses. Almost.

As time passed, Overmier spent more and more time traveling with his wife and less and less time concerned with the affairs of the business. Robert Bainbridge was more than happy to accept more and more of the responsibility for sustaining the ongoing success of the business and reap more and more financial benefits from that success. Those benefits made his wife, Celia, happy, too.

***

Premier Plastics was a plastic-injection molder that specialized in plastic parts for the office furniture industry. And while it was somewhat larger than OM Plastics, it lacked the capacity that OM had to make parts that required three different plastic composites in the same part, a technology that requires larger, more expensive presses—so-called three-shot presses. So, when a large customer changed their chair design that required a three-shot part, Premier had three choices: turn down the business, buy two or three such presses (at $550,000 each and eight-month lead time—time they didn't have), or purchase the parts from a competitor and resell them to their customer.

Sean Weller, the owner of Premier thought perhaps there was a fourth option. He was acquainted with John Overmier and knew that he had MS and was often missing in action at OM. He also knew OM had three-shot presses. Perhaps John might be willing to sell OM Plastics. He decided to find out.

They met at Overmier's home, and while John was inclined to sell and Sean was inclined to buy, neither of them had an idea of the value of OM Plastics. John indicated he had attended a meeting at the last industry conference where a Wall Street investment banker had reported that acquisitions were being effected at four times cash flow. According to his recollection of OM's most recent financial statements, that number was $550,000, which would extrapolate to a sales price of $2.2 million.

"To be candid, John, I don't have $2.2 million laying around. I'll have to be able to convince my bank to support me on this. But my back is up against the wall with this chair part, and I'll need to make a decision fast or sooner. I'll be back to you within a week," Sean said as they parted. And he left with OM's financial statements in hand to see his banker. As he made his way across town to the bank, one thought kept nagging him. OM makes only $350,000 in pretax income on $11 million in sales, which is only, what . . . 3%? Premier made more than twice that.

***

Leonard (Lenny) Johnston was the head of the commercial loan department at Weller's bank. He had earned his title as Executive Vice President by being a smart lender, seeing into good opportunities and through bad ones for over 20 years. Premier Plastics had been a good opportunity for the bank for a long time, so a visit from Sean Weller was welcome.

After Weller explained his predicament, he added his concern about what appeared to be a low pretax income on $11 million in sales. "But," he added, "$2.2 million is only $550,000 more than the three-shot presses would cost, and about seven months' earlier delivery. Buying OM would be a savior in keeping in the good graces of one of my most important customers. Please look this over and tell me what the bank would be willing to do."

Johnston assured Sean he would expedite a decision as soon as possible. As soon as Weller left, Johnston assembled two other loan officers—one of whom was a forensic accountant—to, as Weller had asked, "see what the bank could do."

***

Two days later, the forensic accountant knocked on Lenny Johnston's office door. "I have some answers and one big question," he said after he sat across the VP's desk and opened his laptop. "The answers are that I can find at least $250,000 in positive adjustments to OM's net income in the form of unnecessary or non-repetitive expenses. Since Mr. Overmier takes out a $60,000 salary, the president's salary of $200,000 is duplicated as are his bennies—his car, country club dues, the University Club dues, his first-class air travel, his trip to the International Plastic Show in Frankfurt—which by the way cost the company over $20,000—and on and on. That adds up to $250,000 and change in unnecessary or non-repetitive expenses, which would add $1 million to the value of the company."

"That's the answers; what's the question?"

"Assuming we add back the $250,000 into the net income, we get to a 5.5% net income before taxes return on sales. Premier's net before taxes is 11%. According to what I could find, the industry standard is 9 to 10%. That makes no sense when OM has more sophisticated equipment, can make more complicated parts, and can make regular parts cheaper. Something is amiss here, and I recommend we take a closer look at OM before we make a decision on this loan."

Johnston though for a moment. "But you are saying that at a sale at $2.2 million, the company is undervalued by $1 million. We'd be supporting a $3.2-million purchase with a $2.2-million loan if we underwrote the whole deal for Premier?"

"Well, yes. I suppose so."

"And that's why you're the VP," the accountant thought.

After the accountant left, Johnston picked up the phone. "Sean, Lenny Johnston here. We've done enough preliminary work to indicate we would be willing to underwrite the purchase of OM. But we have a question as to why the net income is below industry standards. I suggest you have an LOI prepared and executed so my people can get into OM and do some due diligence."

***

It didn't take the forensic accountant long to uncover the problem. A time and motion cost study on OM's three-shot presses indicated they could make four parts at a time using three different composites at a cost of $0.39 per part. The parts were high quality screwdriver handles being molded over a blade that OM's customer furnished.

The parts were being molded for Direct Tool Distributors, Inc. for $0.25 each, when the price should have been $0.43. The impact was to affect the bottom line negatively by $360,000 annually and the valuation of the company by nearly $1.5 million.

The deal closed at $4.6 million two weeks after Robert Bainbridge failed so show up for work one morning, and his company car was found in the parking lot with the keys in it.

Out of curiosity, Lenny Johnston asked the bank's legal department to find out who owned Direct Tool Distributors, Inc. A check with the Michigan Department of Commerce indicated the owner was Robert Bainbridge's brother-in-law, and Celia Bainbridge was listed as a member of its board of directors.

***

A few weekends later, Johnston invited David McTavish to join him as part of a foursome in a charity golf outing. They had been involved a time or two in this deal or that, and while they waited to tee off on the par-three seventh hole, Johnston related the story of OM/Premier.

"I thought of calling you in on this one, but frankly the deal was done in about three weeks, largely because of the urgency of Premier to get on with the production of their chair part." Johnston said. "But the strange circumstances of this deal give me pause."

"How so?"

"Would any other bank have poked into the deal enough to uncover OM's hidden value? The difference between $2.2 and $4.6 million is a lot of retirement money. And then, what if Weller had the cash to pay $2.2 or Overmier was willing to take paper and no bank or intermediary was involved? I know I'm preaching to the choir, David. But, I often think, what if . . ."

"That's why we make the big bucks, Lenny. Because we provide a valuable service. In this case, $2.4 million in valuable service. I hope Overmier has expressed his gratitude."

"He has. He is the underwriter for this charity event, which benefits MS and he bought our $250 tickets. Enjoy!"

CHAPTER TWENTY-TWO

"With rare exception, deals done with the buyer's cash are set in stone. All others should include a plan for default. And cash deals done with only the buyer's cash are also a rare exception, so every seller should plan for a default." –Randy Rua

Daniel Harrison was a day laborer working as a finish carpenter when a cousin asked him to furnish the cabinets to remodel her kitchen. His designs were creative, his workmanship was flawless, and the work was done according to the cousin's time frame and budget. When a friend saw the remodel, she hired Harrison to build cabinets in the redo of the bathroom in her master bedroom suite. And that led to another kitchen remodel and yet another, and Classic Custom Cabinets Company was formed.

Over the years, Four Cs, as it became known, grew into a well-equipped woodworking shop with nine cabinetmakers and two installers. Harrison also opened a showroom in a nearby shopping plaza, where he and an associate designed and sold the cabinets and installations.

In most trades in the twenty-first century, good workers are hard to find, and true craftsmen even harder. Harrison began to experience quality issues because of incompetence and people not coming to work on time or at all. Promised delivery dates became harder and harder to meet. At the same time, he needed more help in the showroom as demand for his cabinets was strong.

It was a late delivery to a wrong customer that was the last straw, and Harrison called David McTavish.

Uncharacteristically, three months went by before the first potential buyer made an appointment to see the business. A man with a decidedly Southern accent indicated he was an experienced cabinetmaker and was moving to Michigan. He said the cabinetmaker piqued his interest, and a time was set meet Harrison and see the shop. The buyer showed up nearly 30 minutes late with his family in an older motor home. "Hollister's the name. Henry Hollister, pleased to meet y'all."

McTavish thought Hollister was a bit "rough around the edges," but while he knew and understood the woodworking equipment, he asked very little about the business. Perhaps the write-up of the business McTavish had given him answered all those questions? Surely not!

After a short walk-through of the shop, Hollister got into the motor home, kicked one of the kids off the driver's seat with a cuff and a curse, and followed Harrison and McTavish to the showroom.

At the showroom, Hollister took a cursory look at the cabinets and door-fronts on display but did inquire about the computer software Harrison used to design kitchens and bathrooms or what hardware manufacturers he dealt with.

The meeting was interrupted when a small girl left the motor home, entered the showroom, and after whispering in her father's ear, Hollister asked if the child could use the restroom.

When the girl came out of the restroom, Hollister shook hands all around, thanked Harrison for his time and returned to the motor home with the little girl in tow. The motor home didn't pull out of its parking spot immediately, and as McTavish left the showroom, he could hear Hollister ranting at the top of his voice using words that made McTavish's eyebrows rise. There was obviously going to be hell to pay to whoever misplaced the keys to the ignition of the motor home.

As he got in his car, McTavish allowed how this probably was a waste of time, and he would need to assure Harrison he would continue looking for a suitable candidate to buy his business.

So McTavish was surprised when Hollister called the next morning.

"Hollister here. I wonder if you could recommend a local bank. I'm fixin' to buy that cabinet shop, but I'm not able to pay cash and will need to get a loan on that woodworking equipment." (Aside) "Shut your damn mouth woman, cain't you see I'm on the phone?"

After giving the man a list of local commercial banks, McTavish phoned Harrison to tell him about Hollister's request but also about the behavior over the missing keys.

"I have a bad feeling about this guy and am about to recommend we cut him loose."

"Well," Harrison replied, "We haven't had any other inquiries. Let's wait until we see the color of his money."

"That is entirely your call. But as your intermediary, I'd like to do a bit of investigating and find out just who our Mr. Hollister is or was."

* * *

The Internet can be a wonderful tool. Searching the next day, McTavish learned Hollister was convicted of selling cocaine in 1998 and did time for that, as well as having several misdemeanor assault charges—all in Alabama. The small children in the motor home were apparently from his third marriage, and there was no permanent address.

Before he could call Harrison with the information, Hollister called asking for a meeting as he had some additional questions and wanted to "talk terms."

The meeting was set for the next afternoon at the showroom. When McTavish arrived, Hollister was already sitting at the table, and he came to the point quickly. "I didn't come to waste y'all's time quibbling about your asking price. I've some money for part of it. The City's First Bank's considering a term loan on the equipment, but if we are to do the deal, you will have to take my note and it will have to be subordinated to the bank."

McTavish asked how much of the purchase price would be in personal notes and what interest rate Hollister was suggesting.

"I'm of a mind that $200,000 at 6% would be fair."

It was Harrison's turn. "If I may ask, what is the interest rate the bank is charging?"

Hollister did a slow burn before saying, "8%, but they's a bank. They don't need this deal. You do." And Hollister became more animated. "I ain't contesting your purchase price. 8% is too damn high in these times." He began angrily pounding the table and raised his voice. "I might go to 8%, too, but that's my damn limit. I don't need this deal."

McTavish couldn't tell if Harrison was frightened at the man or angry, and so chimed in, "Mr. Hollister, perhaps you can appreciate that if Mr. Harrison's notes are to be subordinated to the bank, they carry a greater risk than does the bank's loan. That being the case, the higher risk justifies a higher rate."

Hollister sat back in his chair and responded as calm and composed as if he had not just finished yelling and pounding the table. "McTavish, you make a good point. I think we can work something out on interest rates."

McTavish continued, "You might understand how important it might be to look into the background of a prospective buyer, especially if Mr. Harrison is going to take his note as part of the purchase price."

Hollister lowered his eyes and his voice, "So now you know I'm an ex-con. That was seventeen years ago when I was young and foolish and had anger management issues. I paid my debts and have been clean and sober since. I would hope you don't hold a seventeen-year-old mistake against me."

"Where are you living?"

"At the moment in my motor home. But we have an appointment with a realtor this afternoon. We intend to buy or rent something as soon as we find something that suits the missus and her brats."

After Hollister left, Harrison and McTavish huddled, and McTavish was the first to speak. "This guy scares the hell outta me. First, the outburst I overheard about the misplaced keys. I wouldn't be surprised if someone got a good whipping for that. And the table-pounding and yelling over two percentage points. Then there's the criminal history. My gut feeling this guy is trouble waiting for an excuse to pounce. I question if he has the mental stability to run a business. I recommend we send him packing."

"There's certainly reason for being watchful. But there's no one else in the pipeline, and I'm anxious to get out of the cabinet-making business. I had another big quality issue this morning. Unless and until you have another buyer, I would like to see how far this one is willing to go."

Hollister pressed the deal forward, acted as his own attorney, and paid the asking price. Harrison received $500,000 at the close and a $200,000 note at 10% interest, payable in semi-annual installments over five years. He agreed (actually insisted) to stay on as manager of the showroom. "If no one sells, he doesn't make cabinets, and I don't get my note paid off."

***

Four months and one week after Hollister took control of the business, his leadership style, or lack of it, caused all eleven workers in the cabinet shop to walk off the job in a huff. The next day, calls to his cell phone went unanswered, and the motor home was not at the apartment he was renting.

The bank was quick to foreclose on the equipment loan which netted them $76,000 more than the loan, which went to Daniel Harrison. His conversation with David McTavish went something like this, "I got $576,000 for the shop and I can keep the showroom. I can get custom cabinets made for me without the hassle of owning the shop."

"Sounds like you anticipated this."

"I was as wary of the man as you were. But we didn't have another buyer and I figured if I got $500,000 for the shop and could keep the showroom, it would be a good exit. The only thing I missed was, while I didn't think he'd last much past a year, I didn't think he would be out of business in four months."

SECTION TWO

THE EIGHTY PERCENT

CHAPTER 1A

D avid McTavish had made a comfortable living as an M&A advisor. But over an early morning cup of coffee, the day after a deal failed to close, he reflected on the deals that didn't close, the buyers or sellers he didn't help, and the money he could have made on the deals that didn't close. If the national deal closing average of only 20% was correct and the fees he had earned were somewhere around $3 million in the 25 years he been in business, he must have left close to $12 million worth of fees on the tables of the closing that didn't happen. $12 million was a touch more than pocket change and would have made more than a slight difference in his standard of living.

He reminisced about saying that he lost a part of his central nervous system on every deal. "How much of my central nervous system was lost on deals that fell through?" he wondered. "And consequently, how much of my central nervous system do I have left to squander on deals that don't close?"

He reached for a pad of yellow legal paper and began listing all the things that happened that had torpedoed deals. He started with sellers. Sellers who hadn't been prepared to sell, were overly optimistic as to the value of their business, got cold feet, decided to sell at a more opportune time in the future and the future never came. There were sellers who couldn't see detriments to value that were plain to any prospective buyer, sellers who had the wrong professional advisors, and sellers who had no trouble lying under oath and being subject to federal felony penalties on their tax returns but expected prospective buyers to believe their every word as gospel. And there were sellers who couldn't stand the pressure of what it takes in time, money, and nerves actually to close a deal.

McTavish then wrote "BUYERS" on the pad a listed all the reasons why deals didn't close because of failures on the buyer's part. Buyers didn't have or couldn't raise the funds for the purchase price, didn't have good banking relationships, or lacked the knowledge of how to apply for financing successfully. Sometimes buyers lacked proficient advisors, or thought they could "go it alone," or had personality clashes with the seller or someone in the seller's circle. Some buyers couldn't see value. And there were buyers who appeared not to qualify in education or experience.

He did the same exercise for bankers, attorneys, accountants, and advisors.

It was after lunch when he made a listing of some of the deals he couldn't or didn't close and the reasons they didn't come together. He also listed the deals that did come together but had anomalies that could have been avoided and would have saved time, money, and distress.

- James Harrington didn't buy the EDM shop because of the personality conflict of the wives of the principals.
- James Harrington did close on his former employer, Dyno

Machining, but only after an overly optimistic seller as to value had caused him to walk away.

- James Harrington didn't buy the paint gun repair shop because of a misunderstanding over value.
- Sven Anderson lost the sale of his medical equipment company with dire consequences after taking advice from the wrong advisors (a fleece, his employees).
- Richard Dekker failed to purchase Ad Pro from his boss, Megan Sutter, because he was financially unqualified.
- The owner of Rudder Machine couldn't sell because he was overly optimistic as to the value of his company and as result had to liquidate for dimes on the dollar.
- James Harrington did purchase his roll form equipment, but only after his banker nefariously tried to buy his business out from under him, and he had to find a new banker.
- Megan Sutter failed to close on her second transaction for the sale of Ad Pro because she left the process entirely to aides and was not emotionally ready or knowledgeable enough about the details of the transaction to close.
- The Franklin Page/State Street Electric deal didn't happen because there was no schedule of deadlines by which the steps necessary to close the deal were to be completed. The closing dragged out too long, and Page lost interest.
- Eduardo DeLuca left $1.5 million on the table because he failed to use an advisory team in the sale of his interest in the heat-treating company.
- Megan Sutter finally assembled a competent team to sell Ad Pro and was personally and emotionally involved in the transaction—months before she died too early to enjoy the proceeds.
- Don Foster didn't sell when the sale of his computer software company was good. He decided to wait until the selling was

better and "got the cover on his nose."

- Maynard LaRue learned you can set the price of a deal but not the terms when it came time to accept offers for PP&D.
- Henk DeVries learned that the advisory team might need to include someone who could analyze the character of the potential buyers when choosing a prospective buyer when he decided to sell his fastener business.
- John Overmier learned the importance of having qualified people on the transaction team in the sale of his plastic injection molding business.
- Daniel Harrison learned how important it would be to have an exit plan if the deal as constructed for his cabinet shop fell apart.

He was with a 20% failure rate, which requires all the skill, wits, nerves, sleepless nights, and experience as a closed sale (with little or no compensation). This was no way to run a railroad or a merger and acquisition business.

In addition, McTavish was aware that not all his competitors had upstanding reputations, reputations that sullied the profession, reputations that he often had to overcome in convincing potential clients of the need and the value of his services.

Some of these nefarious reputations were well earned. McTavish had followed one business broker who had surreptitiously changed sales documents without red-lining the changes to hide conditions in the deal that were contentious. He knew of one incident where the broker deliberately failed to disclose negative information about the seller's business. Another broker enhanced the valuation of the seller's business by falsely increasing the EBIDA derived from his seller's Income Statement. The term "bait and switch" came to his mind, as did heavy gold necklaces and large pinky rings.

In addition, McTavish was aware of a study by the "Exit Planning

Institute" that found that more than 70% of sellers regretted some aspect of selling, mostly due to unrealistic expectations about LAS (Life After Selling) or the path the business took after the sale.

So, David McTavish decided to change his focus and refine a methodology to educate and prepare sellers for successful outcomes when attempting to sell their businesses. What follows are the principles McTavish developed, tested, and tried out to help sellers and buyers to avoid the frustration of a deal that doesn't go smoothly or fails to close at all; the deals of which we showed examples in Section One.

We don't have a lot of interesting stories in Section Two because for the most part (80% of the time), with some guidance and despite an unexpected pothole in the road, the deals close unremarkably and with (gratefully) a much higher success rate. So, there follows one success story and a story in which you get to decide if it was a success story or not.

Here are some of the roadblocks that prevent transactions from going smoothly to close or crashing before they close:

For a seller:

- Lack of a transition strategy: You do not have a clear way out of your business. You may have some ideas but do not know how to go about it.
- Lack of people: You do not have the team in place both internally and externally to assist you through the transition process.
- Lack of seeking out value building opportunities. You do not see all the opportunities available to create more value in your business.
- Lack of time: You do not feel you have the time to manage the transition process.
- Lack of focus: You do not want to think about transitioning and

would rather put your energy into making the business more successful or enjoying semi-retirement activities.

For a buyer:

- Looking for a business outside your area of expertise: you are not prepared to recognize, adopt, or realize the value of the tacit knowledge embedded in every business.
- Lack of people: you do not have the team in place both internally and externally to assist you through the transition process.
- Lack of knowledge of financing: you do not have the knowledge or experience or the connections that are essential in securing financing an acquisition.

These roadblocks result in only a 20% success rate for business transactions. The typical reasons that acquisitions fail include the following deal-killers:

1) Valuation issues creating unrealistic seller expectations:
   a) Seller stuck on specific price and/or terms.
   b) Seller solely focused on price without considering the terms.
   c) Seller uses inappropriate valuation methods like the 3M Method of Valuation (Make Me a Millionaire).
2) Not hiring proper advisors can cause "deal fatigue":
   a) Attorneys who do not specialize in M&A transactions.
   b) Attorneys who are more interested in billable hours than getting the deal done.
   c) Accountants who do not specialize in M&A transactions.
   d) Lack of a skilled intermediary.
3) Changes in operation results, making valuations difficult.
4) Parties not capable or ready:

    a) Buyer not a legitimate buyer and cannot consummate the deal.

    b) Seller has internal issues that cannot be resolved.

5) Culture issues:

    a) Personality conflicts and ego issues.

    b) Too much emotional involvement–"ugly baby" syndrome.

6) Improper accounting records or accounting irregularities:

    a) Cash basis vs. tax basis vs. accrual basis.

    b) Not compliant with generally accepted accounting principles.

    c) Not compliant with IRS regulations and reporting.

7) Not enough planning in advance:

    a) Seller realized planning is needed and stops the sale.

    b) Surprises that could have been prevented create mistrust.

8) Seller not fully understanding and articulating the "value" to the buyer:

    a) Synergies – not able to tie what the buyer brings to the transaction to cash flow and valuation.

    b) Intangibles – not showing the buyer how to protect, optimize and monetize them.

9) Not addressing or mitigating company-specific risks such as dependencies, lack of diversification, depth of management, pending lawsuits, new competition, emerging technologies, etc.

10) Disagreement over purchase price allocation due to conflicting tax impacts on buyer and seller.

11) Failure on the part of the seller to plan for his or her transition.

    a) Not in control of when and how you exit.

    b) Not ready if and when an opportunity presents itself.

    c) You do not maximize what you put in your pocket.

    d) You incur unnecessary expenses and taxes.

    e) Your family and employees are unprepared for the transition.

    f) You experience unnecessary stress during the selling process.

The tools that follow are designed to overcome these all-too-common deal-breakers. Given that privately held businesses are the number one economic driving force in our economy, it is critical that they transition well.

- Small, privately held businesses account for 50% of the GDP.
- They account for between 60% and 80% of the new jobs created annually.
- They employ about half of all private-sector employees.
- About 80% of all U.S. workers find their first jobs in small business.

It is our hope the tools outlined in the succeeding pages help bring greater success to the transition process and keep small, privately held businesses thriving.

***

A PROVEN PROCESS

All enduring systems are made up of a core group of components that, when implemented, produce desired results. The six key components that have been devised and practiced successfully for smooth transactions are:

The Preparation for Ownership Transition

1. Expectations
2. Right Team
3. Assessment

The Implementation of the Transition Plan

4. Market
5. Negotiations
6. Closing

Expectations:

The goal is to have a clear vision for what to accomplish and having all the members of the team understand and buy into the vision. The expectations should be reasonable and aligned with other key stakeholders and understood by your advisors. The clearer your expectations, the more likely you are to achieve them. These expectations should include what you are trying to accomplish from the transition, what the proceeds might be, what type of buyer and your requirements of the buyer, how much time you are willing to spend, if any, after the transaction to assist the buyer, and what your business needs to look like to be ready for a transition.

Right Team:

Successful businesspeople know how to surround themselves with good people, good people with a wide variety of skill sets. This is also true for a successful ownership transition. You need to have the right people in the right positions. You also need to know what all the key roles are, when to fill those roles, and who will fill them. These include a tax advisor, a transaction attorney, a transaction manager, and to a lesser degree, a financial advisor, an estate planner, an insurance specialist, and a banker. These team members should have experience in the area of transitions, a passion and the time for the often intense schedule that will be required to successfully conclude the transaction. They must be clear about and collectively focus on your expectations. The assistance of this team is critical not only to achieve success, but to allow you to focus on running your business until the transaction is complete.

Assessment:

Sellers must be able to assess their business from the perspective of a potential buyer and the buyer's advisors. These may include an owner-operator who will want to know that the business will be able to generate enough cash flow to pay his or her salary, service any bank debt, pay taxes, and provide a reasonable return on investment. An investor will wish to achieve a desired level of return for the risk taken in comparison with other investment opportunities. The buyer's lender will be concerned with the ability of the business to repay the loan and, if not, what are the risks should the buyer default? That is, are there enough marketable assets to collateralize the loan and/or the guarantees of the buyer? A strategic buyer will be looking for specific opportunities such as new markets, products, capacity, or specific human resources.

Each of these buyers and/or advisors will articulate a version of value in relation to the risk they will be assuming. All sides of a transaction will use one or more of the commonly accepted methods of business valuation. They are:

The Asset Approach: This is the valuation of businesses whose assets have more value than the cash the business generates. It is also sometimes called the Valuation Floor or the Liquidating Value of a business.

The Income Approach: This valuation method determines value based on how much cash flow the business generates. Cash flow is determined by net income before taxes, depreciation, interest, and non-business expenses (such as contributions, owner-inflated perks, rent in excess of market rent, etc.), non-recurring expenses, and/or unusual expenses. Value is determined by capitalizing (multiplying) the normalized cash flow by a capitalization factor. To put it another way, it is the normalized cash flow divided by an acceptable risk.

The Market Approach: This valuation method compares what other companies of similar size and similar industries have sold for.

The Income Approach and the Market Approach are the two most common methods used to determine value. The foundation of both of these approaches is cash flow and risk. Cash flow (often called EBITDA and pronounced "EE-bit-dah") can usually be finitely determined. Risk is a variable that can change with economic conditions. Less risk can be assumed (a higher capitalization multiple) in good economic times and more risk can be expected (a lower multiple) in times of uncertainty or recession.

If one of the team members is not an experienced business appraiser, sellers are strongly advised to add one to their team.

Having wrapped up valuation in a nice neat bow, we will be the first to acknowledge that sometimes there are factors at play, both positive and negative, that preclude an accurate estimate of what the value will ultimately be. Is there a valuator alive who would claim that he or she would have valued Instagram, a two-year-old company with 13 employees and no–repeat–no revenue would be sold for $1 billion (that's billion with a "b")? In fact, a mere few days before the Facebook purchase, "sophisticated investors" bought 10% of Instagram for $50 million, which placed the valuation of Instagram at $500 million, no doubt at the advice of their equally "sophisticated" business valuators on both sides of the transaction.

In the end, it is what an informed and willing buyer will pay and an informed and willing seller will accept that determines that elusive thing called "value." It is the role of the advisors to help the seller (and the buyer) to be informed.

Market:

A market is when there is at least one ready, willing, and able buyer and a ready, willing, and able seller. Unfortunately, when just one of these necessary components is missing, a lot of time, money, and energy is wasted. In our experiences, it is usually a buyer who comes to understand he or she is not able, or a seller who is not ready. These are typically the reason why 75% of all purchase proposals signed by a buyer and seller fall apart before closing. It matters not if the transaction is internal with family, key employees, and management, or the transaction is external involving individual buyers, equity groups, or other businesses.

To avoid these common pitfalls, two things need to be in place. Assuming the seller is willing and able, he or she needs to be ready. By ready, we mean the seller has prepared or caused to be prepared the tools that will be necessary to tell the story of the business. There needs to be a Non-Disclosure Agreement, an overview of the opportunity the sale presents, an executive summary that includes high-level financial information, and a Confidential Memorandum that contains all the necessary information that a buyer would need to put together a proposal that should not change during the due diligence process. An advisor can assist as someone who is familiar with what information should be shared.

Assuming the buyer is ready and willing, it is essential that the buyer also be qualified. Besides the obvious qualification of having the financial resources to make the purchase, other qualifying factors include understanding why the buyer wants to buy a business, what experience the buyer has in this industry or this discipline, what management or educational background the prospective buyer has that would qualify him or her to be successful in this business, if there appears to be a strong personality mismatch between the buyer and seller, and who else in the buyer's immediate sphere of influence will have influence in the purchase decision.

All, except the buyer having the financial resources to effect the transaction, require subjective appraisals. A ready and willing seller may not be objective in appraising a prospective seller. An experienced team typically provides that necessary objectivity.

Negotiations:

The most successful transactions are those that have a process to identify and solve issues quickly. This process is having a team that has an in-depth understanding of both the seller's and buyer's expectations, limitations, and aspirations along with knowledge of the current lending environment.

The first formal component of the deal is the Letter of Intent (LOI) and is usually prepared by the buyer's attorney. The elements of the LOI provide the opportunity to create many permutations of deal structures that could potentially meet the buyer's and seller's needs. It is important that the LOI address, and the parties agree to, all the significant elements up front, or the transaction is prone to fall apart. An experienced team can help by looking at both sides and knowing what each side is anticipating and developing alternatives to make the transaction work.

These are the elements of a transaction that should be included in a LOI to assure a high degree of probability that the deal will eventually close:

- Will this be an asset or stock sale?
  - This defines the overall structure of the deal. Is the buyer

buying the assets of the business, subject to some or all of the liabilities? Or is the deal one in which the buyer acquires the ownership by purchasing all or part of the outstanding stock of the business? The tax implications of these choices can be significant to both of the parties to the transaction.

- What is the purchase price, and what are the terms?
  - The seller will receive the amount of the purchase price in cash at the closing.
  - The seller will finance an amount of the purchase price in the form of a note with specific terms of interest, re-payment schedule, term of the note, and whether there is collateral.
  - Some of the purchase price will be paid in the form of an earn-out, to be calculated periodically based on specific per-formance targets such as sales, gross profit, or net income.
- How will the purchase price of an asset sale be allocated as be-tween the assets and goodwill?
- How much of the net working capital (current assets – current liabilities) will be included in the purchase price?
  - Who gets the incremental cash flow from the time the LOI is signed and the closing?
- Will there be assets retained by the seller?
  - Typically, the seller retains all cash, but there may be some personal items (artwork, vehicles, etc.) that the seller may wish to retain.
- Will there be liabilities retained by the seller?
  - Typically, the seller retains long-term debt and pays it off at the close. There may be other short-term liabilities the seller may retain.
- Will there be a Non-Compete Agreement?
  - This typically will define the number of years and geographic area the seller agrees to be restricted from competing with

the buyer or the buyer's business.

- Will the seller have an Employment/Consulting Agreement?
  - Often the buyer will wish to retain the services of the seller in some capacity.
  - This agreement should spell out the period of time or times the seller will serve and the compensation, as well as the seller's status, i.e. employee or private contractor.
- Is a purchase of real estate contemplated in the transaction?
  - If the transaction includes the transfer of real estate, the price will need to be established as an allocation of the purchase price.
  - In addition, an Environmental Site Assessment may be required and a determination as to who will pay for it.
  - If the real estate is to be leased from the seller, the terms of the lease must be established.
- Will an earnest money deposit be required and, if so, how much?
- Will there be an Exclusivity Clause in the agreement?
  - An Exclusivity Clause defines a period of time that the seller cannot talk to another prospective buyer of the business. Sometimes the seller will require the buyer not to seek out other businesses to purchase.
- Will there be a time limit on the buyer's due diligence process?
  - The LOI will spell out the process, timing, time limit, and who may be included in the process—on the side of the buyer and also on the use of the seller's employees.
- What will the closing date be?
- Whose attorney will be charged with preparing the closing documents?
  - It is important that this be decided at the time of the acceptance of the LOI so that time and money are not wasted by opposing attorneys both preparing the closing documents.
- Will there be other financial and or legal issues that will need to

be addressed prior to closing?

The more definitive the LOI, the better understanding both parties will have of the eventual deal. The more the advisors understand the needs, goals, and aspirations of the parties, the more the LOI can be adjusted if needed as the process proceeds to achieve those goals.

Closing:

In our experience, 90% of the efforts of the buyer, the seller, and their advisors go into closing the deal. Very often, failure to close the deal is because there no plan, no schedule that addresses the closing issues. An effective closing schedule is broken down into the following elements:

1. Closing date – This date to be effective should be no more than 90 days from the execution of the LOI. It is the date by which time all of the items needed to close must be completed.
2. Responsible Parties – The top of the schedule identifies the parties who will be responsible for completing elements need for the closing.
3. Closing Elements - The items that need to be completed in order to close.
4. Due Diligence – This section outlines the main due diligence areas and all the steps necessary to complete the due diligence.
5. Financing – If financing is required, this section covers all the requirements a lender will need to approve the financing indicated in the transaction.
6. Legal – This section outlines all of the legal documents that need to be created and be ready for distribution, approval, and signing on the closing date. Some of the common documents are:

   a. Asset Purchase Agreement or Stock Purchase Agreement

   b. Seller financing documents (notes, security agreements, mortgage, Guaranty)

   c. Other documents (Bill of Sale, Consulting Agreement, Assignments, Covenants Not to Compete, etc.)

For each item, the responsible party and the due date will be inputted, and typically it is the responsibility of the intermediaries on each side to follow up on the members of their team to see to it the schedule is strictly adhered to. This will be made easier if a Buyer/Seller Work Group schedule is prepared with the names, phone numbers, and email address of the respective team members, the lenders, and others who may have responsibilities to complete the close.

If the buyer requires outside (bank) financing, it becomes one of the largest elements of the efforts required to close, and a buyer will do well begin the loan application process as early as possible in the closing process. The lending institution may require most, if not all, of the following information:

1. The Loan Application
2. Personal background and Financial Statement of the Buyer
3. The Financial Statement of the buyer's business, if applicable:
   a. Current Profit and Loss Statement, current within 90 days of the application
   b. Profit and Loss Statements and Balance Sheets for the past three years
   c. A detailed one-year projection of income and an explanation as to how the projection will be achieved
4. A list (names and addresses) of all ownerships and affiliations in which the buyer has a controlling interest and other concerns that may be affiliated by stock ownership, franchise, and

proposed merger or acquisition.

5. Business Certificate/License – your legal status of doing business.
6. Complete loan application history whether successful or not.
7. Copies of signed federal income tax returns – both personal and business for the past 3 years.
8. Resumes of each buyer if more than one.
9. If applicable, a brief history of the buyer's existing business, its origin, progress to the present, and its challenges.
10. Existing building lease if the buyer's business rents the real estate it occupies
11. Additional Information about the business to be purchased:
    a. Three years Profit and Loss Statements and fiscal year-end Balance Sheets.
    b. The buyer's projections of the business's trajectory for the next 1-3 years.
    c. Previous three years' federal income tax returns.
    d. Proposed Bill of Sale including terms of the sale (Signed LOI or final draft of Purchase Agreement).
    e. A/P and A/R Aging list.
    f. Detailed inventory list and pricing.
    g. Equipment listing.
    h. Equipment Appraisal.
    i. Real Estate Appraisal (if the Real Estate is part of the sale).
    j. Environmental Site Assessment (if Real Estate is part of the sale).
    k. Documentation of patents, trademarks, long-term supplier contracts, long-term sales contracts, etc.)
    l. List of all existing liens to be discharged.

As one can see at a glance, transactions for the sales of businesses are not for the faint of heart nor to be taken casually by the stout of heart. One can also see the need for a professional, qualified team to advise and run interference and perhaps why, without this assistance, the failure rate is in the 80% range.

In fact, the closing process is where the wheels can come off a transaction even when the preparation is perfectly executed. This is because there is an intense period when all of the advisors, who all have varying opinions and different perspectives, are trying to protect their clients.

The cumulative effect of additional legal conditions demanded by one side or the other's attorneys and the financial analysis loaded on by CPAs proves too much for many M&A transactions to survive. It is also not uncommon for either the buyer or seller subconsciously to sabotage what they've been working towards for so long. The closing process is a lethal place for even the most promising of transactions. Both buyers and sellers should be prepared for the following challenges:

Reality Sets In

At some point a switch is thrown in the mind of the buyer or seller. They come to realize that everything they've been considering from a theoretical point of view is becoming reality. For the buyer, it may be the difference between looking at spreadsheets and legal documents to thinking about facing the first staff meeting in front of people he doesn't know and who don't know him.

For the seller, it's a shift from having conversations about selling to preparing to tell employees that they will have a new boss, or that the business conceived in love and passion some time in ancient history will no longer bear his name or his influence.

Anxieties and uncertainties about the future have a powerful effect of distracting either or both parties from their ultimate goal.

The Devil in the Details

All too often, details are not seriously considered until late in the process. As the reality of the transaction sets in, the importance of details becomes inflated. Tax implications, working capital adjustments, employment agreements, assumptions used in financial models, the unexpected loss of a customer or employee, a rise in the price of a purchased component—all of these unexciting or unexpected developments are suddenly approached with a new sense of importance or urgency. In M&A transactions, small details can translate into large changes in risk and valuation, or buyers can be tempted to use these "surprises" as leverage to materially alter the terms of the deal, even the price.

Emotions

The marriage analogy is appropriate in M&A transactions because finding a good match is important. The lives of the buyer and seller will change drastically when the transactions happen in ways they couldn't imagine. So, it should be no surprise that emotions run high and feet get cold as the big day draws near. When jittery nerves are present, it only takes the slightest unexpected turn of events to throw the entire transaction into jeopardy.

These challenges cannot always be avoided, but their implications can be controlled, if not reduced, by:

- Having established reasonable expectations for both the prospective seller and buyers.
- Accumulating the right professional team.
- Analyzing and agreeing on what a prospective deal might look like.
- Developing and choosing among qualified prospects.

- Implementing a closing scheduler.
- Having a team that is focused on the same goal.

***

To summarize, while it will be helpful and even appropriate to outline proven steps to take to make acquisition transactions have a better chance for success, it has to be acknowledged that every transaction is different. Different kinds of businesses, different personalities of sellers and buyers, different levels of experience and competence in advisors, accountants, and lawyers, changing tax laws, different economic conditions, and different reasons for selling and different reasons for buying are all either impediments to or conditions for success.

While the reasons for transaction failure are legion, these proven steps, administered by experienced and knowledgeable advisors, are proven to improve dramatically the chances of closing the transaction. And as rewarding as a successful closing is, alleviating the stress by following a clearly delineated path shepherded by experienced professionals may be equally important.

So even though getting out is harder than getting in, sellers and buyers should know the resources you may need as a buyer or a seller are available to you. This book may be one; experienced advisors will be another.

Call us if you need us.

CHAPTER 2A

"Here's how it is supposed to work and how it does . . . mostly." –Randy Rua

J eff Harmsen was a college graduate engineer who felt stymied in his first job out of college. He thought the things he learned on the robotics team at the University of Michigan could be applied creatively at the packaging machinery company where he was working. But his boss constantly reminded him that tried and proven "old school" methods would be the model for their creativity, creativity that Harmsen thought was passé fifteen years ago.

So, after two years, he left to start his own business, Robotics Technology, Inc. (RTI).

Fast forward 15 years, RTI is a leading company manufacturing specialty robotic equipment for a wide range of applications, with automotive leading the way, to circumvent the wages and benefits of $72 per hour for assembly-line workers. The growth was nothing short of phenomenal, and in 2011 it reached $23 million in sales. Jeff Harmsen proved to be an extraordinary engineer—near

JAY M. BYLSMA AND RANDY RUA

genius. No fewer than 32 patents had been granted for innovations that were his "brain-children," and RTI was internationally known not only for their creativeness but also for the simplicity and durability of their designs. But as creative as Jeff Harmsen was, he was not a businessman. His only attention to financial matters could be synthesized into one question, "Did we make money this month?" And to his sales department, all he cared to know was "How many jobs in the pipeline"? He left the daily operations of sales, human relations, finance, and production to his team of vice presidents so he could immerse himself in creating new and better ways to eliminate the human element in mass production.

He also devoted considerable time and funding to a new-found passion—sponsoring and mentoring the local high school's competitive robotics team, which—under his coaching—became very successful among the tops in the state.

His call to David McTavish came after his CPA firm uncovered a significant embezzlement during their annual audit. "I haven't paid close enough attention to the operation of this business. Frankly at this level of sales, managing it is over my skill set. Things are happening at the highest levels without my knowledge while I'm on the shop floor making robots. There is a level of details I'm not interested in or competent to handle. It's time for me to think about getting out and getting free while the getting is still good. What do I need to do to sell?"

McTavish took his playbook along when he met with Harmsen. "First, we will need a concerted effort to make RTI as saleable as possible. A prospective buyer will want to know the business can continue without you as your creativity has been the driving force in its growth. In addition, a buyer will want to confirm that you have best-practice procedures in place for managing the business. They will need to see evidence that your patents are properly assigned to the company and that you don't rely on any major customers who may leave or major suppliers who may be problematic. You will no doubt be asked to sign a Covenant Not to Compete with the buyer.

"We will need to value RTI so you can have an idea what a transaction might net you. We will need to assemble a team to assist you and make this as easy a transaction as possible. That will include a transaction attorney to assist on the legal side of things and a CPA to help you with the tax considerations.

"At some time soon, you will need to meet with your management team to tell them of your decision to sell and the reasons. Your family should be told as well. This is so that people can transition into the sale without shocks or surprises. I can help you with those announcements.

"After the team is assembled, the valuation is agreed upon, and the consequences of possible terms of sale are discussed, it will be my responsibility to seek out, screen, and qualify potential buyers for your consideration. This will be done as discreetly as possible, but there will need to be some plant visitations.

"And of course, there will be a contract covering our relationship and responsibilities and the associated fee."

$$***$$

The valuation came out at $12.5 million. McTavish, the CPA, and Harmsen discussed the implications of the possible terms and agreed McTavish should offer the business as a stock sale with negotiable terms, but preferably cash. Harmsen signed McTavish's Representation Agreement.

The team took shape with McTavish as the head. The law firm RTI used for patent applications had an M&A department with whom McTavish had worked successfully in past transactions and that he respected. RTI's CPA firm was well known for their expertise in M&As and had worked with McTavish on the valuation.

With the team in place, McTavish met with the management team of RTI to announce the decision to sell and answer their questions. Harmsen had decided that $2 million of the purchase would be distributed to key employees in recognition of their service to him. That helped the announcement of Hansen's intentions to sell to be met with enthusiastic approval.

With those preliminary steps out of the way, McTavish set about finding qualified buyers. He made several calls, one of them to James Harrington of CORE Industries.

"David, I'm very interested, in fact, I've often wondered if RTI might be for sale. But I know you, and if you are true to form, you will have three or four buyers nipping at the heels of this deal. I would like that if I were the seller, but I am not interested in getting into a bidding war. I'm a cash buyer, and I'd rather do an asset deal, but a stock deal is not out of the question. I would be willing to give RTI a serious look if you will agree to let me be the only looker, and I ask for only two weeks to make a decision to buy it or not. Do we have an agreement?"

Because of their long-standing relationship and the quality of CORE Industries as a buyer, McTavish said, "I'll give you three weeks. I'll send over their financial statements and other pertinent documents by courier tomorrow."

In two weeks, Harry phoned McTavish with the news CORE was interested pursuing the deal and that an LOI would follow in a day or two.

The LOI was simple: a cash deal at $12 million, closing to be in 75 days, existing management team to be offered one-year contracts, Harmsen to sign a five-year Covenant Not To Compete for

YOU JUST CAN'T MAKE THIS STUFF UP...

$500,000, with $100,000 payable at closing and four successive payments of $100,000, each payable on the anniversary dates of the closing, and the deal contingent on satisfactory completion of a reasonable program of due diligence to be conducted by CORE's CPA firm. Sale documents to be prepared by RTI's attorney.

McTavish called a meeting of both RTI's and CORE's advisors and distributed the LOI and a Closing Schedule with responsibilities carefully assigned with due dates. CORE's CPAs asked to move their due date for completion of the due diligence back by two weeks, indicating a conflict with necessary educational licensing course requirements for the staff that would be involved.

During the preparation for closing, three potential potholes came to light. One was that Harmsen insisted on the advice of his CPA that the payments for the Covenant Not to Compete began on the first anniversary of the closing to avoid subjecting that first payment to the high tax rates the sale would generate in the closing year. CORE agreed.

The second was that an Environmental Site Assessment revealed the presence of a contaminant in the one of the collection drains in the floor of an indoor shipping dock. The contaminant was not identified. CORE insisted RTI pay for an investigation as to the composition of the contaminant. The investigation determined, with a 95% degree of certainty, that the contamination was hydraulic brake fluid. The cost to clean up the drain and the disposal of the contaminated soil was $16,950, which RTI agreed to assume and have completed by closing.

Third issue was CORE's attorney insisted on certain guarantees regarding product warranties on equipment sold prior to closing. While admitting much of the equipment and systems produced was cutting-edge technology, the RTI team balked. They asked CORE to rely on their well-documented warranty history and their reputation for customer satisfaction. A compromise was reached when it was agreed that $250,000 of the purchase price would be set up in an escrow account to pay for any warranty claims that occurred within a year of the closing. The remaining balance, if any, would be distributed to Harmsen.

The day before the due date of each scheduled item, McTavish communicated with the party responsible for completing the item in question. While there were delays of a day or two here or there, his follow-up was effective in keeping things on track.

The closing was held on the scheduled date.

At the celebratory dinner with his team members and their spouses at a posh restaurant, Jeff Harmsen asked everyone to raise a glass to his team for a job well done, within budget, and on time, "like a well-designed and well-oiled . . ." here his voice choked up a bit, ". . . and well-made robot! I'm forever grateful. Here's to my team!"

"Hear, hear!"

"And ladies and gentlemen, this weekend I will be mentoring Michigan City High School's robotics team as we compete in the state finals . . . and win!"

"Hear, hear, hear!"

CHAPTER 3A

"Sometimes what appears to be a good deal isn't what it appears to be, depending on one's perspective." –Jay M. **Bylsma**

We have one last story to tell. We'd like to use James (Harry) Harrington, the president of CORE Industries in a fictionalized setting of a true event, a merger or acquisition gone well—or maybe bad, you decide.

$122 million in sales is a large machine shop, and CORE Machining (now CORE Industries, Inc.) had become one of the largest operations of its kind in the Midwest. There were six separate state-of-the-art locations: one for CNC machining, one smaller location for laser cutting, a large roll-forming center, a large-capacity metal-stamping facility, a smaller EDM operation, and an engineering/ machine shop that had recently been purchased that manufactured robotic equipment—CORE had been a big customer before the purchase and continued to be thereafter. The divisions were networked via the Internet by a sophisticated manufacturing/

accounting software package. Each had a plant manager who had relative autonomy but who operated under operating budgets for expenses and capital expenditures. An eighteen-person sales force reported directly to Harry, as did the six plant managers who oversaw a total of 1,250 employees.

The growth had been financed by an IPO in 2012, and CORI was the symbol on the NASDAQ. The IPO had raised $54 million for 75% of the then-outstanding stock. James Harrington retained 25% ownership, valued at $18,000,000 – 1,500,000 shares at $12/share. You can't spend stock certificates, but Harry didn't need to. He lived very comfortably on his $850,000 in annual salary and bonuses, thank you very much. And at 62 years old, in three years he would retire and try to spend the 75-cent-per-share dividend the CORI stock was paying.

Fast forward two years. On Thursday morning, Harry was preparing for the CORE quarterly board meeting to be held the next day when his secretary interrupted his thoughts.

"There's a Mr. Manning on the phone. He says he has an urgent message and must speak to you."

"Thank you, Barbara. I'll take it," and he picked up the phone. "James Harrington here."

"Mr. Harrington, I'm Allen J. Manning. I'm the president and chairman of Parkland Industries, I'm sure you've heard of us. We like to say we're the largest metal benders in the country. Our New York Stock Exchange symbol is PMB. I'm calling to tell you Parkland is going to offer your shareholders $18.50 per share for their stock and pay a $1.00 dividend. We think this is a generous offer. I'm sure you are aware that's a $3.50 premium over today's opening. We hope this takeover can be friendly. I know your board meets tomorrow. I'm doing you the courtesy of telling you of our intentions in anticipation of any public announcement so you can have time to give this proper consideration at your meeting. I'm staying in town at the Hilton. My cell number is . . ." And Mr. Manning clicked off.

Harry didn't put the phone down; rather, he dialed a familiar number. When the phone he called stopped ringing, he heard a familiar voice. "David McTavish."

"David, James Harrington here. I want to engage you to find out all you can about Parkland Industries. Symbol PMB. I just got a call from their president and chairman. They are about to launch a hostile takeover of CORE. He is offering $18.50 a share with a $1.00 dividend. We have a board meeting tomorrow. Is your schedule such you can help me out?"

"For you it is. Let me get busy, Harry."

Harry got busy revising the meeting's agenda.

***

Harry had McTavish's report in hand at 7:30 the next morning. In summary, it read, "Long history of takeovers with a bit of a checkered past. Existing officers have 'retired' early. They have drained cash-rich companies (which yours is), cashed out over-funded pension funds (which you have), have a history of fights with the IRS, and have liquidated some acquisitions with asset values greater than the purchase price. But their shareholders love them—160% market value increase in the past five years."

At the board meeting, the officers and one outside director voted "No" on the motion to accept Parkland's offer. Two outside directors voted "Yes" and explained why. "We understand that as officers of the company, this deal represents change and uncertainty for your employment and futures. But we represent the shareholders and frankly, this is a good deal for them. To show that we deliberated in good faith, I move that we counter-offer with $22.50 per share and a $1.50 dividend."

"That's $7.50 over the market price and double the dividend. The company's not worth that," Harry observed. "He'll never accept that, but maybe this will signal that we're not for sale."

The motion passed. Harry went to the phone and told Manning of the counteroffer.

Manning's response was, "Welcome to the Parkland family of companies. Here's what the press announcement will say: 'The Officers and Directors of CORE Manufacturing Company are pleased to announce . . .'"

Harry was stunned. The room was silent. This did not have a good feeling. That his quarterly dividend check would now be $562,500 and that his net worth had increased by $11 million in the past 60 seconds didn't cross Harry's mind.

***

James Matson was CORE's VP of Finance. He was the one who was told to send all CORE's available cash ($6 million) to Parkland, to send a letter to all CORE's suppliers that invoices would henceforth be paid in 120 days, and to send the pending tax return that had been prepared by CORE's Big-Eight CPA firm to Parkland's tax department. He was also the one who watched the over-funded pension fund be reduced by the amount of the over-funding and the excess be funneled off to Parkland. The fact that Parkland had doubled his salary and given him a golden parachute should he decide to leave was of little comfort.

When Harry told Matson that Parkland had instructed him to fire CORE's Corporate Secretary, David Trudor, Matson was stunned.

"Why?"

"Because . . ." (you just can't make this stuff up) ". . . he's a Baptist and as such answers to a higher power."

"Harry, I answer to at least two higher powers. The same one David Trudor does, and my family. I think I should save Parkland the trouble of firing me." And with that, he walked out into the October sunshine without cleaning out his desk but with the feeling he had cleaned out his soul.

By the time he got home to tell his wife, Harry had called twice and left a message both times. "Please call me as soon as you get home."

Matson dialed Harry's private number. "Thanks for calling, Jim. Listen, I know how you feel. This merger was a huge mistake, but for the sake of the employees, I'm sticking around to hold it together. When I told Parkland you'd quit, they instructed me to get you back for whatever it takes. Apparently, they have no one to step into your shoes, and they tell me their form of operating budget that is due in February is extremely complex. I'll need you to prepare that.

"We go back a long way, Jim, and I'm imploring you to come back, at least until the end of February and this operating budget is finished. Besides, the revised tax return came back from Parkland today, and I need you to interpret it for me. As a friend, please?"

So, for a $50,000 bonus and an extension of this golden parachute from one year to eighteen months, Matson came back and stayed until February 28 at 5:00 PM and the operating budget was complete.

The tax return was problematic. The $5.2-million liability CORE's Big-Eight accounting firm had calculated was miraculously reduced to $2.1 million. A trip to the Big-Eight firm's tax department with the revised return got incredulous looks and the advice that the return was fraudulent and to sign it would be a federal felony.

Parkland's response to that was, "It's okay to sign it and not to worry. We take care of our own."

Harry sent the tax return back to Parkland, and someone there was made an officer of CORE and signed the return.

***

On March 1, Matson woke up a free man. He had eighteen months at full pay and a $50,000 bonus check to tide him over until he found a new job. Or not to find a job. The dividends on his CORE stock was enough for him to consider the possibility of retiring. The first thing he did that day was list his home with a realtor he knew. It was time to get out of Dodge.

It was in the second week of March that he got an invite to have lunch with David Trudor, the former Corporate Secretary of CORE who had been fired because he "answered to a higher power." Trudor suggested an out-of-the-way diner Matson had never heard of. It would be good to meet and catch up.

But Trudor was about more than catching up. In hushed tones, he relayed that at a State Bar meeting, he chanced to be in on a conversation in which a first-year lawyer in a silk-stocking firm, after too many trips to the open bar, bragged that one of "his" clients had successfully taken over a local listed company by buying off two of the outside directors for $100,000 each. They were coached by the buyer's CEO to suggest a counteroffer with a 50% premium over the opening market price, which they did. The unsuspecting seller countered, the buyer took it, and avoided a hostile takeover. Moreover, they covered the premium they paid for the stock by raiding the company's cash and over-funded pension fund.

Trudor sat back in his seat and asked, "Do you know of any other company that acquired a listed company in this town that fits that set of facts?"

Matson didn't say anything for a long time because he couldn't think of anything to say. He also couldn't think of anything he wanted to eat. He would've ordered a stiff drink, but the diner didn't serve alcohol.

***

Matson chose not to tell his wife Sarah what he learned at the diner until three weeks later when Harrington called. "Jimmy, Harry here. Listen, something's come up and I need your help. Apparently, the Los Angeles office of the SEC has received a complaint that there was something improper about the CORE/Parkland deal. Mr. Manning has hired an investigative law firm out of New York to see if there is anything to this. This firm wants to talk to the directors. I know this turned out to be a bad dream for all of us, but would you be willing to talk to this lawyer soon? Manning wants to get these baseless charges behind him as soon as possible."

"I'm not sure I have anything to say. When do they want to meet?"

"They'll be in town Thursday morning."

"Let me think about this. I was hoping that after the end of February, I wouldn't have to spend one more second thinking about Parkland."

"I know how you feel. Let me know as soon as you decide, either which way."

When he hung up the phone, he told Sarah everything. Her response was, "What are you going to do?"

"Call a lawyer I know."

He dialed a number and when the person said "Hello," Matson said, "I really enjoyed our meeting at the diner. When could we do that again soon?"

"How about tomorrow?" David Trudor answered.

"See you there at noon?"

***

They met at the same table, and Matson relayed Harry's request for Matson to meet with Mr. Manning's "investigative attorney."

Trudor was more than a little concerned. "Since I learned what I heard at the ABA meeting, I did some checking, and Manning and his crowd are not ones to mess with. The cruel joke at Parkland is that if you cross Manning, you take a long walk off a short pier at his beachfront mansion at high tide and disappear without a trace. He has a security detail comprised of ex-Navy Seals.

"So, to start with," Trudor was deadly serious, "Don't use your home phone or your cell. Go to Wal-Mart and get what's called a burner—an untraceable phone. Then don't call from your home. It's on the market, right?"

"Yes."

"Has your realtor had any Open House showings?"

"Two, one just last weekend."

"You can expect your house to be bugged as well as your phones tapped. Any strange cars hanging about in your neighborhood?"

"None that I've noticed, but just a frigging minute. Isn't this all a bit extreme?"

"Jim, Mr. Manning is not going to go to jail or let his reputation be tarnished and will do anything or anybody to prevent that. And he has the power to make sure of it. Trust me, you are playing in the big leagues here."

"So, do I meet with this attorney of his?"

"You are in a bit of a predicament. If you refused to see the attorney, you will seem to be hiding. If you meet with them, you better be a very good liar."

"What would you do?"

Trudor thought for a moment. "I'd call Harry back and tell him you are willing to meet with this attorney, but you would like Harry to be present and meet in Harry's office. That way you will have a witness to what you say and it's on company property, so it's company record and can be subpoenaed, if necessary. My bet is they won't agree to that. If this is not on the up and up, this is one way to find out."

***

The next morning Matson made the call. "Harry, James Matson. I have nothing to add to the Los Angeles inquiry. But I'm agreeable to meet with this attorney. It would give me great comfort if you could be there as well. So how about Thursday at your office at ten o'clock?"

"That would be great. I'm appreciative of your willingness to come in and speak to these gentlemen. Thursday at ten o'clock it is."

Within twenty minutes, Harry called back, "Jim, I'm sorry. I should have checked my calendar. I'm not available Thursday. Would you be willing to meet with this attorney at the Marriott on Thursday at noon? They are offering to buy lunch."

"I'm disappointed you can't be there Harry. Without you there . . . I don't know. Let me get back to you."

Matson walked into this backyard and used the burner to call Trudor. "You were right, Harry says he can't meet at ten o'clock on Thursday after he said he could. The attorneys want to meet me alone at the Marriott. Now what do I do?"

"You meet me at the diner for lunch."

"I think I need to meet somewhere where they serve alcohol."

When Matson drove out of his driveway to meet Trudor, he noticed a black Suburban with tinted windows parked at the end of his cul-de-sac. He couldn't see if there was anyone in it.

***

After they ordered, Matson told Trudor about the Suburban. "I'm starting to see hitmen on the streets and hear clicks on my landline. This is no way to live. What is going on here?"

"As I said, these people play for keeps. Have you decided if you're willing to meet with Manning's attorney?"

"It seems to me I will appear to be guilty or hiding something if I don't meet, and I'm afraid I might let something slip if I do. And by the way, need I remind you, I was not on the giving or receiving end of a hundred grand to swing the merger. There is no justice for me to be on the hot seat like this. I feel like I'm on the other side of the table from the mafia."

Trudor let that comment sink in for a moment, and then said, "You are. This is not the Italian Mafia; this is the Corporate Mafia. If they think you had anything to with the SEC complaint or you know about the fix, you may well have to be taken care of. And they won't leave a trace." Trudor's look was intense.

"So what should I do? What would you do in my position?"

"I would meet with the attorney and this is how I would do it . . ."

***

Matson arrived at the Marriott promptly at noon on Thursday. As he entered the restaurant, he scanned the room until he saw the two PIs (private investigators) Trudor suggested he hire and whom Trudor had coached. At the same time, an immaculately well-dressed elderly man approached him with a warm smile and stuck out his hand, "Mr. Matson. My name is Hiram Wiesenbalm, but my friends call me 'Hy,' and I invite you to call me 'Hy' as well. Mr. Wiesenbalm is my ninety-eight-year-old father, and I won't be Mr. Wiesenbalm until he passes, God bless him. Our table is over here." The overly kindly gentleman guided Matson to a table occupied by a much younger man.

"This is my young associate, David Bierman. I take him along to schlep the briefcases." Bierman rose to shake Matson's hand. They sat down, and Matson pretended to read the menu while Wiesenbalm explained the purpose of the meeting.

"As you might imagine, Mr. Manning is deeply distressed over the false accusations coming out of Los Angeles. Los Angeles of all places. Who could have guessed? My firm, we specialize in representing folks against the SEC, has been hired to get to the bottom of these charges. I am instructed to let the chips, if there are any chips, fall where they may. Manning is most anxious to learn if there is any truth to the allegations and take appropriate action if action is warranted . . ." Wiesenbalm droned on with platitudes about Manning as if he were the fourth person of the Holy Trinity while young Mr. Bierman buttered his second roll.

Just when Matson started to relax and enjoy his salad, Wiesenbalm adroitly turned the subject to, "How are Sarah and the children? You have two boys and a girl if my facts are correct. I understand your oldest is a very good basketball player. Perhaps there is Division I scholarship in his future, mmh? And your father, recently retired from Plaxton. Is he enjoying his retirement? I've thought about retiring, but I don't play golf like your father."

No questions, just statements to let Matson know they knew

more about him than he knew about them. If the old man was trying to intimidate, it was working on Matson's stomach.

After Wiesenbalm appeared to tire, it was Bierman's turn, and his focus was whether Matson knew if anyone of his fellow officers at CORE were unhappy with the merger or had an axe to grind with Harrington—the person who benefited most financially from the merger. Innocuous questions, dancing around the elephant in the restaurant. Matson relaxed a bit when it occurred to him that they couldn't ask him the correct questions about "the fix" without tipping their hand that there had been a fix.

Just before the waitress came to inquire about dessert, Wiesenbalm stopped Bierman's questioning. "I think you can tell our associates their services won't be needed. They can be excused." Young Mr. Bierman rose from the table, walked to a table near to where Matson's P.I.s were seated, and whispered to one of its two occupants. Whereupon they picked up their check and left the restaurant—two of the most thuggish-looking men Matson could remember seeing outside of the movies, except no ill-fitted suits. These wore Armani. The message was clear, very clear. This was the big leagues, James Matson was at bat, and Parkland Industries was pitching.

Wiesenbalm was saying, "We have just a few more questions, as a favor and for some privacy, I suggest we adjourn to our room—room 345—it's a suite actually. Would you be willing to oblige us? Fifteen to thirty minutes, no more. We are so thankful for your cooperation so far . . ."

Trudor had warned this would happen and what to do if it did. As Matson stood, he caught the eye of one of his PIs and nodded. "Hy, if you wouldn't mind, I would like to find the restroom before I go up. Too much iced tea."

When the P.I. approached the adjoining urinal, Matson said only, "345."

As the P.I. turned as if finished, he said, "You know what to do."

Matson had been carefully instructed by Trudor and the PIs. "You need to establish proof you were in their hotel room. Here's what you do. Tell them the restaurant's restroom was being cleaned, you need to use theirs. In the bathroom, put your wallet in the waste basket and cover it with toilet tissue. When you are being questioned, stand by the window so the PIs can get a picture of you from outside. When and if you leave, find an excuse to return to the bathroom and retrieve your wallet."

"Is all this really necessary?" Matson wanted to know.

Trudor had been emphatic, "If they decide you should be taken care of, their story will be that you left the restaurant in the company of a good-looking young woman. We need to be able to prove you were last seen in their room. If we have photos of you in their room and the maid finds your wallet, their alibi goes away. And so do they."

***

When Matson got to Room 345, the real questioning began, but not before the attorneys for Mr. Manning let it be known they had information from his high school transcript, his college transcript, his scores from the CPA exam, the ages and birthdates of his wife and children and enough more to make Matson's head spin and put a real scare in him. But he had an advantage. He knew they couldn't ask the right questions without tipping their hand that there had been a fix.

When they ran out of questions, Matson asked to use the bathroom again, got his wallet, and walked out of Room 345. As he walked toward the elevator, he passed one of the PIs who was standing at the ice machine. "All clear?" he murmured.

"All clear," Matson answered, and he began to breathe normally.

When he got home to a relieved wife, there was no black Suburban at the end of the cul-de-sac, and there were no more clicks on his landline.

***

In June, David Trudor noticed a small article in the *Wall Street Journal* citing an AP source that Mr. Allen Manning, President and CEO of Parkland Industries, was cleared of an allegation of impropriety in conjunction with the CORE/Parkland acquisition that had been under investigation by the Los Angeles office of the SEC. The story quoted Manning as being pleased at being found innocent of these specious charges and that justice had been done on his behalf, blah, blah, blah.

You just can't make this stuff up, he thought.

Made in the USA
Middletown, DE
22 August 2024

59049862R00099